With my very best wishes,
Richard Williams

I Left My Hat in Moscow

I Left My Hat in Moscow
Seeking God and Finding Him

A Christian Apologetic
by Richard H. Williams PhD

I Left My Hat in Moscow
Richard H. Williams
Published by Aspect Design, 2023

Designed, printed and bound by Aspect Design
89 Newtown Road, Malvern, Worcs. WR14 1PD
United Kingdom
Tel: 01684 561567
E-mail: allan@aspect-design.net
Website: www.aspect-design.net

A copy of this book has been deposited
with the British Library Board.

ISBN 978-1-912078-34-9

To my wonderful wife Linda, who has travelled this road with me. For her love, gentleness, wisdom, cheerfulness, humility and support in every way.

Contents

Acknowledgements ix

Introduction 1

Part One: Apologetic Evidence: Seeking God and Finding Him

CHAPER 1. Early Days 7

CHAPER 2. School 13

CHAPER 3. University 19

CHAPER 4. Conversion 22

CHAPER 5. Dad 27

CHAPER 6. Moving On 29

CHAPER 7. God the Matchmaker! 35

CHAPER 8. Desert 39

CHAPER 9. Restoration 43

CHAPER 10. St John's Church's Overseas Mission 51

CHAPER 11. The Fall of Communism 54

CHAPER 12. Romania 58

CHAPER 13. The Republic of Moldova 63

CHAPER 14. Russia/CIS and the Former Soviet Union 75

CHAPER 15. How Can We Find God? 90

Part Two: The Evidence From Christian Revivals

CHAPER 16. Revivals Impact upon Wales 103

CHAPER 17. Previous Revivals and Their Effects 110

Part Three: Apologetic Evidence: Old Testament Prophecies Fulfilled

CHAPER 18. Jesus the Messianic Fulfilment 117

CHAPER 19. Four Specific Predictions 126

CHAPER 20. The Dead Sea Scrolls 135

Part Four: Apologetic Evidence: Science And God

CHAPER 21. Famous Scientists and Christians 145

CHAPER 22. The Big Bang 152

CHAPER 23. Fine-Tuning of the Universe and Planet Earth 154

CHAPER 24. Evolution and Natural Selection 161

CHAPER 25. The Age of the Earth and Universe 171

CHAPER 26. Biological Evolution Compared with Evolutionism 177

CHAPER 27. The Book of Genesis and Scientific Discovery 182

Bibliography 197

Acknowledgements

There are many people who I wish to thank for bringing this book into being. My editor John Miles M.A. PhD has done wonderful work which is deeply appreciated. My friend Roy Allen has been a great help in reading and proofreading the script and making helpful comments.

For the book itself, my warm thanks go to the following for ensuring the accuracy of what has been written: for St John's building project, Liz Berry; for Romania, Les and Dot Tidball; for Moldova, Mark McCormick and Stephen Williams; for Russia/CIS and the Institute for Bible Translation, Dr Borislav Arapović, Dr Marianne Beerle-Moor and Dr Vitaly Voinov; for the science section, the Revd David Talks.

There are many other people who have helped and encouraged me in many ways. I wish to thank all of them. For those precious people with whom I have worked in St John's Church, Colchester, and who have also prayed for me in this work over many years. I wish to acknowledge with grateful thanks the love, prayers and support of Jenny Woodhouse, and the late Florence Peak; also those many with whom I have worked on behalf of Romania, Moldova, and Russia/CIS who have taught me so much. They have been a major part of my Christian life.

I am also most grateful for the following friends who have helped me on my Christian journey. These include the late Revd Maldwyn Griffiths and his wife, Bidi, who have been wonderful friends, especially during my student days. Also to those who have encouraged me to write this book and the Revd Bill Lewis who has been a mentor throughout my Christian life. He once said to me 'Richard, one story is worth a thousand arguments.' Also to the Revd Brian and Hilary Nicholson, a former vicar of mine and his wife, who first suggested that I write this book.

The views expressed in this book are my own, and do not necessarily reflect the views of the above or of those people mentioned in the text.

Please note

All scriptures quoted in this book are from
the New International Version (NIV).

Introduction

It is a real joy for me to write this book on Christian apologetics. The word *apologetics* comes from the Ancient Greek word *apologia* (ἀπολογία), and in essence refers to a defence, an explanation, or a rebuttal, as used in the Greek legal system. This is my personal contribution to the defence of Christianity. The apostle Peter wrote the following to Christian believers, 'but in your hearts revere Christ as Lord. Always be prepared to give an answer to everyone who asks you to give the reason for the hope that you have.' (1 Peter 3:15.)

In our mainly secular Western world, there are multitudes of people who have lived, and died, without believing in the God of the Bible, simply because they have thought or have been taught 'where is the evidence that God exists?' One such person was the twice awarded Nobel Prize-winner Professor Frederick Sanger who became an agnostic, saying 'he lacked hard evidence to support his earlier religious beliefs.'[1] There is, however, a vast body of evidence – in fact we are surrounded by it – provided that we look in the correct places. This, then, is my attempt to look into some of this evidence. Apologetic evidence can take many forms. I will let you into a secret, I am a great fan of such approaches, and I have read many books in this field, not least the works of C. S. Lewis and

1. Denise Gellene, 'Frederick Sanger, 95, Twice a Nobel Laureate and a Genetic Pioneer, Dies.' *The New York Times*, 20 November 2013. https://www.nytimes.com/2013/11/21/science/frederick-sanger-two-time-nobel-winning-scientist-dies-at-95.html

Alister McGrath. A major part of this interest of mine stems from my own scientific background. I like to look into the evidence for things, and I try to grapple with big themes. In this book, I will concentrate on just four of the many valid kinds of evidence to make my case for the existence of God. Each of these four sections is intentionally written as a stand-alone section for the reader.

The first of these is my own testimony of how I searched for and found God; then subsequently how I was guided into Christian service, including missionary work. This has mainly been in the former Soviet Union after the downfall of Communism. The second kind of evidence relates to Christian revival. I am from Wales in the United Kingdom, and the last major revival in Wales came to my local village of Letterston, and to other places close to where I lived. I aim to show that revivals are life-changing Christian encounters with God, not simply emotionalism, and they have continuously revitalised the Church over many centuries ever since the first revival which was the birth of the Church on the feast of Pentecost, as recorded in the New Testament in the book of Acts chapter two. The third kind of evidence explores prophecies in the Old Testament relating to the coming of the Messiah, and how these were literally fulfilled in the person of Jesus Christ many centuries after they were written. My fourth kind of evidence is in the area of science and Christianity. These two stand together as two truths about creation and about God. These are most certainly not in conflict. This has long been an interest of mine, as I have trained and worked as a biological scientist for over forty years.

I hope that this book will go some way in showing that God is real, that the Christian faith is not a myth, a fairy tale or something that some people hold on to in spite of the evidence. Genuine belief in God is because of the evidence, not in spite of it, and the root word for faith comes from the Latin word *fides*, similar to the word *trust*. In other words, it is evidence-based and is not simply the product of human imagination.[2]

My hope and prayer is that this book will help others to know personally the one who loves us, who wishes to live his life in and through us, and to make his home with us. It is with a humble spirit that I write this, so that others may come to know the one true God and experience true life, both now and for eternity. The Scriptures say 'For God so loved the world that he gave his one and only Son, that whoever believes in him shall not perish but have eternal life.' (John 3:16.)

2. Peter J. Williams, *Can We Trust the Gospels?* Crossway Books, 30 November 2018.

PART ONE

APOLOGETIC EVIDENCE
Seeking God and Finding Him

Chapter One
Early Days

This is the account of my search for God from a young age, and it is an integral ingredient of this book on apologetics. The story of God's immanence (that he can be personally known), and of his loving desire to be in intimate fellowship with every human being on Earth, is a universal one and is most certainly God's intention. I share my own story and reflections in the knowledge that what I am saying is completely normal and not in any way unusual in the Christian life. This story is just one of myriads that have been lived over the centuries, and are just as true today. Together they show the many ways in which God works in human lives. I write my own account because this is the one that I know best.

This, then, is my testimony to the faithfulness of the Christian God, the one for whom I searched and found. He has led and graciously used me, with others, for his greater purposes in ways that I never anticipated nor thought could be possible. This has included missionary service, with others, in helping in the re-building of the Christian church in the former Soviet Union; mainly since the downfall of Communism, and God's very specific training. His calling of me for this purpose was long before it was even on my mind. I have observed that God seems to specialise in calling ordinary, often rather inadequate people for his greater purposes rather than the 'high and mighty'. Perhaps ordinary people are more likely to give the glory and credit to God rather than to themselves. They are more likely to pray and depend upon God working rather than rely upon themselves and their talents. Ordinary people being led and used by an extraordinary God seems to be what usually happens, and my story is simply an explanation of how God did this in my own life, as just one example of countless untold stories out there.

A little of my own background to set the scene. This section is not an autobiography as such. Instead, this is an account of my life in relation to God and his gracious dealings with me, simply to show that God is God, that he is actively at work in our daily lives, and that every single one of us can come to know him if we know where to look.

I was born in March 1950, into a farming family from North Pembrokeshire, a Welsh-speaking part of West Wales just ten miles from St Davids in the parish of Mathry. Dad was a farmer, as were most of his family. Dad's roots in that area go back several hundred years. Mum was from Camborne, Cornwall, and was also from a farming family. Her maiden surname was 'Eva', an unusual Cornish name from an old Cornish family who, like my dad, had lived in the same area for hundreds of years. How on earth did my parents meet, being that they lived so far away, in relatively isolated communities? Perhaps uniquely, in contrast to today's eclectic range of online and other dating methods, their particular 'dating agency' happened to be the Pigs Marketing Board! I have certainly never come across any other couple who met like that. Dad's cousin and mum's dad were both on their committee. They became good friends, and their families came to know one another. That was in 1946, just after the Second World War. My parents were married a year later, in 1947. I have an older sister, Alicia, who was born in 1948.

We have a large extended family. Dad, besides his two sisters, had thirty-six first cousins, and fifty-two second cousins (we spent an afternoon counting them!), the majority living in Pembrokeshire.

Also, my sister and I have twenty-one first cousins. Both of our parents' communities were quite similar, both had a shared Celtic history, a certain geographical remoteness, and were rural and closely knit. Our family was quite privileged compared to most, as this was early post-war and farming was enjoying a period of prosperity. Alicia and I were born into that environment, just two miles from the beautiful Pembrokeshire coast. It was, in many ways, idyllic. I think it was very brave of my mother to agree to be uprooted from her close family and strong community, to be transplanted into my father's. She was only in her early twenties, and it was certainly a giant leap into the unknown. My father's family were very kind, but still, this was a massive undertaking on her part. This then is my family background, which I trust sets the scene a little.

Both of my parents went to church, and it was a rich blessing to be brought up in the Christian tradition. We went to our local Anglican parish church in Mathry, the Church of the Holy Martyrs, every Sunday; which even in the early 1950s was rather unusual. We regulars were few in number, with less than a dozen of us attending each week. What was also exceptional was the depth of my father's Christian faith. Besides his family and farming, the church was his great interest and passion throughout his life. He was the churchwarden of Mathry Church for well over thirty years (from his twenties), which meant that we came to know a lot of the clergy from St Davids Cathedral, named after David, the patron Saint of Wales, which was only a twenty-minute drive from our home. My parents were 'church' rather than 'chapel', and certainly through the regular Sunday worship, with the Bible being read, great hymns based on Holy Scripture, and the beautiful 1662 Prayer Book liturgy, we had a good basic grounding in the Christian faith.

As this is a book about apologetics, I would like to share two examples of godly people who impacted me early on because of our link to St Davids. One was the Reverend David Jenkins (who, by the way, wasn't the one who became the Bishop of Durham), a young man in his thirties who came to lead services in Mathry during a period when we were between vicars, known as an interregnum. He came and had breakfast with us every Sunday before the service, so I came to know him. He was a lovely man, and he was a Christian missionary. He had recently served in Yokohama, Japan, as a chaplain to the Mission to Seamen, and the fact that he had gone all the way to Japan to share his Christian faith had an apologetic impact on me. In other words, I realised and appreciated that this man cared sufficiently about the things of God to go to the other side of the world and live as a Christian in a non-Christian country. Japan was a country that practised Shintoism and Buddhism.

Another great man who led our services during this interregnum was Canon Rhys Davies. He was also a man of deep spirituality, in his late seventies, whom I later came to know well. I asked him what prompted him to become a vicar. These questions always interested me. He explained that in his youth he had served in the First World War, in the Battle of the Somme. On the first day of the battle, there were three of them in a trench, with him in the middle. They were hit by a shell, and his two friends on either side were killed outright, but he was left totally unscathed. He felt strongly that this was divine intervention, and his Christian calling arose from that. This story also had an apologetic impact on me. Surprisingly, perhaps, given all this spiritual 'voltage' around me, I still didn't *know* God in the sense of having a personal relationship with him or anything like that. Indeed, I didn't think it was even possible to really *know* God in an intimate way, but I did realise that God could intervene now and again, perhaps *in extremis* as in the Battle of the Somme, but I was unlikely to have to face anything like that.

Obviously, we did many other things as a family. Dad worked

hard on the farming side and he enjoyed this, plus the social aspects of life in our rural community. We also had a caravan which we kept at Whitesands Bay, near St Davids, between the months of April and October. We had our own place in Sandy Lane, right by the beach. It was in a lovely spot and we greatly enjoyed the beach, the walks, the views and also the company of many of our relatives and friends, particularly those who lived near St Davids.

There are many stories that could be told, but I will limit these to just one amusing anecdote. This was around Mum's cooking and her hospitality. She loved entertaining, and on one occasion we somehow managed to squeeze fourteen people around the table for a wonderful caravan afternoon tea. Mum said at one point, 'I am sure that I made a Victoria sponge. Can anyone see it anywhere?'

The answer was 'no'.

Then, a few minutes later, my great-aunt Rose, then aged eighty-five, said, 'wait a minute, I think that I may be sitting on something soft.' And sure enough, she had inadvertently sat on the sponge! We laughed so much, nobody more than Great-Aunt Rose, and it took us some time to get over this highly comical event.

During these early days of my life, I became interested in gardening and in plants generally, rather more than in farming. I had my own patch in our large garden, mainly growing flowers. Mum was interested, and she encouraged me. Her speciality was dahlias. She grew a massive range including cactus, decorative and pom-pom varieties which she entered in the various local horticultural shows which were thriving in the 1950s and 1960s at Mathry, Hayscastle and Croesgoch, to name just three. She quite often won the first prize and a nice silver cup when she entered the dahlia competition. It was great fun and these local shows brought out the competitive streak in us all.

Robert, one of my first cousins, is the same age as me, and he lived on the next farm, not far from our local village, Castlemorris. We did most things together during our early years, and attended the same schools until the age of thirteen, in Mathry, Fishguard and Selwyn House, a preparatory boarding school in Begelly, near Tenby. It was great to have a good friend of the same age, and we had a lot in common. We got into a fair number of scrapes of one kind or another which I won't go into here, not least because it would take up an entire book on its own.

Chapter Two
School

Until the age of nine, I went with my cousin Robert to two local primary schools, Mathry and Fishguard. I think we learned a lot at Fishguard, it was a fairly strict regime and we were certainly given plenty of homework. I learned Welsh and could speak it for a short while. I also remember learning a little about our local Welsh history, particularly the bluestones of the Preseli Hills (only eighteen miles away) and that for some reason they were used in the building of Stonehenge, the world-famous prehistoric monument in Wiltshire, erected around five thousand years ago. I also learned that another major historic event, the last invasion of Britain, occurred in Fishguard in 1797. This was an attempt by an army of 1,400 soldiers from France to invade the UK. This action was foiled in a major way by Jemima Nicholas, a local heroine, who, upon hearing of the invasion, armed herself with a pitchfork and led a group of women to round up twelve French soldiers. The soldiers were then held as prisoners overnight in St Mary's Church, Fishguard. The French surrendered shortly afterwards in Fishguard.[1]

At the age of nine, Robert and I were sent to Selwyn House Preparatory School, Begelly, near Saundersfoot in the southern part of Pembrokeshire. Again, I could write a book about our interesting experiences there. We had now entered the realms of private

1. Ben Johnson, 'The Last Invasion of Britain', Historic UK. Accessed 15 February 2016, https://www.historic-uk.com/HistoryUK/HistoryofWales/The-Last-Invasion-of-Britain/

education, where pupils are prepared for the Common Entrance to Public Schools, taken at the age of thirteen. That was the route arranged for us, for some other cousins of mine and children of our parents' friends. This was a fairly relaxed regime in many ways and pretty good-natured. I remember learning quite a lot from the head, Mr Stuart Cobb, who taught us Latin and history. I also remember Mr Brewin, a decorated Second World War army major, who taught us maths pretty well, including some elusive subject called trigonometry. Besides we farmers' sons, a number came from Tenby, Pembroke and several whose parents were stationed at Castle Martin, a local army training base. In Selwyn House, due to its relatively small size (there were only around thirty of us, all boys), we were all in sports teams.

I remember being in the first XI for cricket, even though I was normally 'out for a duck' and missed all the catches which came my way when fielding (or just getting out of the way, as a matter of health and safety). Then there was the rugby first XV, which I felt was rather more fun. I ended up being on the wing, and then a prop. I think that one of the highlights was our 'away' fixtures when we paid regular visits to other Welsh preparatory schools such as Abermad (near Aberaeron, Ceredigion), Llandovery and Christ College, Brecon. These were full days out. They were enjoyable, and I think I can truthfully say that we often won these matches or indeed, that we most certainly 'held our own.'

There were many highlights in our Selwyn House experience and the school did provide a decent all-round education. I remember that we had an annual garden competition, judged by Mrs Fraser, the elderly mother of Mrs Cobb. We knew that she couldn't see well at her age, so we made sure that our plants had nice fragrances giving us a better chance of winning! Every Sunday we walked to Begelly Church for their morning service, and we were given one of those brass threepenny bits to put into the collection. The rector also taught us Scripture, but I think he missed the opportunity of doing this properly and we ended up being told ghost stories which rather missed the point.

I heard a few years later that he had frightened the local Mothers' Union with something similar; he was publicly reprimanded by the then Bishop of St Davids, the Rt Revd John Richards, a distinguished theologian and former missionary to Iran. We took our Common Entrance examination at the age of thirteen. It didn't seem too difficult, and my parents had carefully chosen a good school. The following term I found myself at Malvern College, a fairly well-known public school beside the Malvern Hills in Worcestershire, together with my friend William from my old school. I was placed in house number seven and my housemaster was Denis Saunders, a strict, but very decent, Yorkshireman. I quite enjoyed my Malvern experience in many ways, and I certainly made good friends there. Actually, I cannot really fault the school. I did have quite a severe anxiety problem that had plagued me since early childhood, but in those days these things weren't discussed at all. Somehow, it was just a case of muddling through. This was a pity because some sort of child guidance or counselling support would have greatly helped and enabled me to prosper there rather more than I did.

The head, Donald Lindsay, taught me history, and I enjoyed his lessons. For Latin, I had Mr E. C. Kennedy (known by his initials as 'ECK'), a distinguished classicist and older man with extremely thick spectacles. He seemed almost blind but enjoyed a bit of banter. His lessons were always fun and I sometimes deliberately put my work bag in his pathway in order to trip him up. He didn't seem to mind at all, and he took it in good spirits, including throwing my bag out of the window, which we both knew was thoroughly deserved. Notwithstanding all this, I learned quite a lot of Latin!

We had compulsory Combined Cadet Force (CCF) every week, and I decided to join the army section. I enjoyed dressing up in army kit and 'square bashing'. I later joined their arduous training section which involved a number of weekend hikes in the Brecon Beacons, some night operations and a week in Bangor, North Wales. We also had the opportunity to regularly shoot targets with a .303 rifle, which had an effective range of 550 yards and a maximum firing range of 3,000 yards. Why on earth they entrusted these to immature fifteen-year-old boys, I will never know!

We were encouraged to join societies and clubs, of which there were many. I joined the photographic club, the numismatics society, took up woodwork and learned to play the violin. The latter was a weekly event taught by someone called Lady Maureen Dunbar, who was the wife of the director of music. She was a lovely person, and I learned long after I left the school that she was, in fact, the foster sister of C. S. Lewis, the famous Christian writer, being the daughter of Jane Moore whom Lewis looked after and lived with after his friend's death in the First World War. C. S. Lewis and his brother had both previously been pupils at the school.

I am sorry to say that my woodwork skills were pretty hopeless. Over a two-year period, I managed to make a cheeseboard which took a whole term, a breadboard that took two terms, and an extremely unstable magazine rack, which took me a whole year! Mr Shaw was our teacher. I remember him saying to the class after my two-year stint: 'You probably won't believe this, but Williams is probably the best woodworker that number seven has ever produced!' I took that as a bit of a compliment at the time, but I really think that he meant the opposite!

At the age of fifteen, I chose science subjects rather than arts. It was a pity that we had to make this important choice at such a young age. So it was biology, physics and chemistry for me from then on. In due course, I joined the biology sixth form, from where many went on to study medicine. The school was fortunate, in those days, to have its own nature reserve. This was a place called Hope End, near Colwall, a short bike ride away, and I spent many happy hours there. We had an excellent biology master named Arnold Darlington. He was a truly inspirational teacher, and I owe a lot to him. It was he who directed me towards my future career. I first became interested in plant research by doing some pollination experiments on *Berberis* and *Symphytum* at Hope End, with some fascinating results. I was awarded the school's Natural History Prize for this work, which was a great encouragement at the time and significant for my future career decision.

What about the religious/Christian aspects of life at school? Did I find God? Was it humanly possible to know God? As young men of thirteen to eighteen, I can truthfully say that we probably had as many discussions about God as we did about other personal matters, including sex. This may seem surprising in this day and age when looking back more than fifty years. We had compulsory chapel on alternate days, with voluntary chapel in between, which I nearly always attended. Additionally, there were house prayers on alternate evenings before bed.

Some things stand out for me; there seemed in my mind to be a real openness about the things of God for we young men and amongst the masters. I was really searching for something or someone greater than myself, particularly in view of my anxiety issues. I was confirmed by the Bishop of Worcester in the College Chapel when I was fourteen. I was hoping that something would happen God-wise on that occasion, but I didn't experience anything and neither did my friends. I remember one evening, after house prayers, going to my housemaster's study and asking, 'Sir, do you genuinely believe in God?' Mr Saunders was immensely kind and treated me like a fully grown adult in our heart-to-heart conversation. He said that, quite honestly, he didn't know. It was a good and frank thing to say. For whatever reason, I did not encounter God in any personal way during my school tenure. At that time, I didn't know that God, in whom I believed, could personally be known. That was completely outside my experience, and I think probably outside the experience of almost all my friends and fellow members of the school.

Chapter Three
University

My school enabled me, above all, to determine what I really wanted to do for a career. I was very fortunate to have been sent to a good school that exposed me to so many opportunities, to work out what I most enjoyed and was good at. This, for me, was a scientific research career. After obtaining the required grades I was accepted by my local university, Aberystwyth, to study agricultural botany. Aberystwyth was only sixty miles from my home in Pembrokeshire, so that gave me the opportunity to easily travel home to see my family and friends.

I enjoyed the summer of 1969, not least because on 20 July my parents and I were able to watch, totally enthralled, the first manned landing on the moon, and marvel at how this could humanly be possible. It was one of those 'where were you when' moments, which perhaps occurs just a few times in a lifetime. I remember that week going outside, looking up at the moon, and thinking 'Wow!'

That October I began my course at Aberystwyth University. I stayed in a hall of residence, Pantycelyn, for the full three years. This enabled me to meet with, and enjoy the friendship of, many fellow students. There were 250 of us in our accommodation, studying many different courses. It was all very enjoyable, and I grew in personal confidence. We were kept busy in our studies with lectures and practical classes almost every day from 9.00 am to 5.00 pm. The agricultural botany department was very well run under the leadership of Professor Hugh Rees, who had previously served with distinction as a Lancaster bomber pilot during the latter part of the Second World War. He was awarded the Distinguished Flying Cross (DFC), and then later became a prisoner of war in Stalag Luft One until its liberation in 1945. We were given an excellent grounding in genetics, plant breeding, plant physiology, plant pathology, statistics and agronomy. Other subjects were also part of the course, such as pure botany and biochemistry.

I have to say that I loved the whole experience, and somewhat came out of my shell during that time. However, my anxiety problem, coupled with clinical depression, did make things difficult. I was afflicted two or three times a year for several weeks at a time; periods where I just couldn't function or sleep. It was only much later when, after a bad spell in my early postgraduate days, I realised that medical and other help was available. Thankfully, these days mental health is given a higher priority, and it is a great help for those with such conditions to know that they are not alone. Celebrities, amongst others, speaking out about their conditions have done much to remove the stigma, raising public awareness so that these illnesses are nothing to be ashamed of and effective treatment is now widely available.

Our department was closely integrated with the former Welsh Plant Breeding Station (WPBS), situated near Bow Street, close to Aberystwyth (now re-named the IBERS).[1] For example, there was a jointly run two-year master's (MSc) course in plant breeding which attracted students from many countries. The director of the WPBS at that time, P. T. Thomas, was also a professor at the university. Both the WPBS and the department were held in high international regard, and Professor Hugh Rees was later elected as a fellow of the Royal Society (FRS) for his work on chromosome genetics and evolutionary changes in chromosome organization.

1. Aberystwyth University, '100 Years of Plant Breeding'. https://www.aber.ac.uk/en/ibers/about-us/history/100-years-of-plant-breeding/

It occurred to me early on in my student days that I would like to work towards a PhD at the WPBS, mainly because this is a research degree, and I wished to have a career in plant or crop research. I had taken a particular interest in crop physiology and was introduced to Dr (later Professor) Des Hayes, who encouraged me to work with him. We had many discussions about which particular topic to study. I wanted to study spring barley because this was very widely grown at the time and any findings in this area could well apply to other cereal crops.

The research would be aimed at finding out what determines grain yield in this crop. Once determined, this would enable the plant breeder to select more efficiently for higher yielding crops. I took my finals in June 1972 and obtained my BSc in agricultural botany, together with a postgraduate research scholarship from the (then) Agricultural Research Council, to study my chosen topic, starting in October 1972.

During my undergraduate days, I went to church every Sunday, worshipping at Holy Trinity Church. I was also an active member of the university's Anglican Society. None of this was particularly demanding, but I found it of interest and made some friends there. There was an active Christian Union, but no one I knew went there and it was outside of my experience. One matter puzzled me during my teenage and student days; it was simply those words of Jesus to 'love the Lord your God with all your heart and with all your soul and with all your mind,' as the first and greatest commandment, the second being to love your neighbour as yourself, as recorded in Matthew 22:37–40 and elsewhere in Scripture. My subconscious question was a simple one; how is it possible to love God if you don't know him? This question was answered later in my experience, as recorded in the next chapter.

Chapter Four
Conversion

At the age of twenty-three, I started training to be a lay reader in the Church in Wales. Having been a regular communicant church member (baptised at age one, confirmed at fourteen) and having moved in those circles since a very young age, I thought that I knew as much about knowing God as was possible in this world. I liked what I had heard and seen about Jesus, and I was keen to 'do my bit' for God and the church. I wrote to the Archdeacon of St Davids, the Venerable B. Alec Lewis, who was the diocesan warden of lay readers. He was a very nice man, humble and very encouraging. Despite my young age, he accepted me onto the course. This involved some study, regular meetings with four other trainees in Carmarthen, and reading/helping to take services in my local church in Mathry. I actually quite enjoyed all this.

At the same time I was, as explained, a postgraduate research student at Aberystwyth University and was fully involved in university life. This included an active social life around my hall of residence, called Cwrt Mawr. I had a good friend called Mike, a chemistry research student whom I had known well since our first year as undergraduates, and both he and I became friendly with two girls, Christine and Catherine. Mike started dating Christine and a little later I started dating Catherine. Although Mike and I went to church regularly, what we didn't know was that these two girls were 'real Christians' who knew God in a way that we didn't.

They most certainly had something that we lacked. Unbeknown to us, they were earnestly praying for us both to 'become converted'. I remember one occasion when Christine said to me, 'Richard, are you sure that you ought to be training as a lay reader?' I was a bit miffed at this comment, to be honest, but it struck home. This would have been around the autumn of 1973.

I am convinced that what happened next to Mike and me was entirely due to their prayers. We began moving into some of their friendship circles; people who were a little too earnest about God, or so we thought. This included going to prayer meetings and Bible studies. We both felt very uncomfortable at these events, thinking (correctly) that we were lacking in some vital area. Also, a number of people gave their 'testimonies' which I had never heard being spoken before. I remember one person, Don, explaining to a large gathering how he had tried to kill someone with an axe and had spent time in prison, where he had 'found God'. I have to say that this was different from the rather more comfortable 'Ang. Soc.', the University's Anglican Society, which I had faithfully attended for over three years. I kept on meeting many more of these 'rather earnest' people. Even more disconcerting was that a number of them were Anglicans, having been 'converted' in their mainstream Church of England churches and who had come to Wales as students.

Events for me and Mike started to 'heat up' after that. In November, Dad informed me during one of our frequent phone calls that he had been diagnosed with high blood pressure (the remedy in those days was simply to try and lose weight by cutting down on bread and potatoes), with advice to return for a further blood test after a year. In the new year of 1974, Catherine and I ended our relationship. A week later, Dad developed pneumonia and pleurisy. This was serious, but apparently not over-serious. As my home was only a two-hour drive (south) from Aberystwyth, I went down every weekend in my faithful Morris 1100 car to stay with Mum and Dad. It was good to see him and to have quite long chats about many things. These were precious times. He was always very kind to me and very encouraging about my chosen career. One day he said, 'Richard, could you go to Haverfordwest library and get me a couple of religious books?'

'Yes, of course.' I borrowed two, one of which (intrigued by the title) was called *Holiness* by J. C. Ryle.[1] I gave one to Dad and kept *Holiness* to read on my own.

This is what happened to me; I got stuck into reading this intriguing book, written by Bishop John Ryle, the Anglican Bishop of Liverpool from 1880 until 1900. I had never before read anything like it. It was tailor-made for me! He explained how it is possible (often normal) to be baptised, confirmed, or even be a vicar or a bishop and still not be truly converted. He quoted a lot of Scripture to back up what he was saying, and he got me hooked. One verse especially 'spoke' to me. It was 'make every effort to live in peace with everyone and to be holy; without holiness no one will see the Lord', (Hebrews 12:14). He pressed home that holiness is God's goal for our lives and without this transformation, we cannot be saved. I realised that in no way had I even begun to be 'holy'. I was totally undone. I asked for God's forgiveness there and then in my bedroom and immediately experienced an inrush of the Holy Spirit. It was an extraordinary and unexpected supernatural encounter with God. I just knew in that instant that God had fully entered my heart and that I had received something totally new, which included immense peace.

It is difficult to describe, but I knew that I was changed forever. The following day, being a Sunday, I went to Mathry church and

1. J. C. Ryle, *Holiness: Its Nature, Hindrances, Difficulties, and Roots*. The Banner of Truth Trust, 2015.

everything came alive for me: the Bible readings, the hymns, the 1662 Prayer Book. They seemed fresh, with new meaning. Within a few hours, I had gone from being 'someone on the outside looking in' to 'being on the inside' with my standing before God. It was a joyful experience and something that I didn't know was possible until it happened. It was only later that I heard and understood that I had received a new life spiritually and that this has a sound Scriptural basis. I go into this further, and how anyone can receive this, in chapter fifteen. No one needs to wait ten or more years as I did; this offer of new life is open to all. It doesn't matter how good or bad we are, it is free and it can be instant. Finally, after ten or more years of real searching, I realised that I had found God! My underlying question of 'How is it possible to love God if you don't know him?' had now been answered. He can be known! I went back to Aberystwyth that evening and I met up with Mike, who had been away the previous week. Before I said anything, Mike said, 'Richard, I need to tell you something.'

This is what happened to Mike. In the previous week, Mike had read the book *From Witchcraft to Christ* by Doreen Irvine. He had been away doing his postgraduate research at the Atomic Energy Research Establishment (AERE), the Harwell Laboratory, near Harwell, Oxfordshire. One evening, within the AERE and whilst in a room on his own, God did something very similar for him. Mike said to me, 'Richard, I have come to know the Lord!'

I just said 'Snap!' and gave him a hug. Amazingly, Mike and I had become converted, quite independently of each other, through different means, and both during the previous week, within a few days of each other! Later, when we were both aged twenty-six, we completed our research theses within fifteen minutes of each other and again unknowingly! A little later I gladly served as best man at his and Christine's wedding. I was at the threshold of a new life in Christ and had the joy of knowing that, from then on, God's hand was guiding me.

What had I missed in my church experience before my encounter with God? I am convinced that in my case there were two crucial things. First, there needed at some stage to be a personal response to the claims of God. That is, a full acceptance of Jesus Christ in my heart as my Lord, and receiving God's free gift of salvation for me. Secondly, for me personally to accept Jesus Christ as the all-sufficient substitute for my sin through his death on the cross. Only Christ's sacrifice on the cross saved me from my sin and definitely not any good things or church membership of mine. Somehow, the teaching I had received during my church experience was inadequate on these two counts. It was present, maybe assumed, but it was not emphasised within my particular church tradition.

I believe that I was very lucky, if that is the correct word, to have received these powerful experiences of God. It was God's great grace to me. I am, however, acutely aware that there are many faithful Christians from different church traditions who have simply not had this kind of experience. For many, their conversion may have been far more gradual, perhaps occurring over many years. For others, it may not yet have happened. In the United Kingdom only around six per cent of the population go to church regularly, and if you are one of these then I salute you; you are heroic and faithful. The more immediate question for us all is where are we now in our Christian walk? In chapter fifteen I go into further detail concerning the A, B and C of entry into the Christian life. It would be good to go through these simple steps if, as in my case, you are unsure or have not yet received the assurance that you would like concerning your standing before God.

Chapter Five
Dad

This is what happened to my dad. Throughout January, he gradually began to recover from his illness. We spoke a lot about the Christian faith, and I explained to him my experience, which gave him joy. I was also really impressed by the way Mum looked after Dad during his illness. She was up day and night and did a wonderful job of nursing him. One night, later in January, Dad had an awful nightmare about dying. Mum comforted him and gave him a hot drink. He immediately went off to sleep and had the most beautiful dream that he had ever had. It was a dream about a lovely man with a beard who came into the room and said, 'Please don't worry, I will always be with you.' Dad felt so good, and he talked about it several times. I was also pleased that Dad appeared to be getting better from his illness. I returned as usual to Aberystwyth the following Sunday evening.

Around 9.30 am on Wednesday 6 February, whilst working on my research project in Aberystwyth, a call was put through to me. It was Mum; 'Dad has had a bad heart attack. Please could you drive home?'

I said, 'How bad?'

Her answer was 'very bad.' I arrived home just after midday and received the confirmation that Dad had died. It was such a shock. He was only fifty-eight and our assumption had been that he was on the mend. Events over the following days were rather a blur and seemed very unreal. We chose a particular hymn for the service that we knew meant a lot to Dad, 'The Church's One Foundation.' Its opening verse is beautiful:

> The Church's one foundation, is Jesus Christ her Lord;
> She is his new creation, by water and the word:
> From heav'n he came and sought her to be his holy bride;
> With his own blood he bought her, and for her life he died.

Dad was 'spiritually ecumenical' in his thinking, and was very accepting of Christians from other traditions. Not least, his father and forebears were Welsh Baptists, originally from Tretio village near St Davids and his mother was an Anglican. We had the funeral service and people were immensely kind, but obviously we had experienced a great loss that would take a long time to come to terms with. There was a lovely write-up about Dad which included the following anonymous tribute from a neighbour:

> When I arrived in Pembrokeshire twenty-five years ago I had the great good fortune to have Tom Williams as a neighbour, and very soon as a friend too. I learned great respect for his farming skills and appreciation of his unfailing kindliness. He not only knew everyone but one felt that he cared about everyone. He was a rare man – a man about whom no one spoke without affection. He was modest and did not seek office, but he gave his help and service without stint or hesitation to the Church, to the farming community, to his neighbours and to his wide circle of friends. We are all the losers when such a man passes and our deep sympathy goes to his wife and family in their tragically early loss.

For me to have been converted just before all this was a real grace from God. It most certainly gave me the strength to cope, and I hope also to have been of some comfort to others during this difficult time.

Chapter Six
Moving On

My research supervisor, Dr Des Hayes and the staff at Aberystwyth were very helpful during this time. I was able to return to my research work three weeks after Dad had died. I was so advanced in my studies by this time (year five) that I did not feel any compulsion about going home to farm or anything like that. I just carried on as normal, with the addition of returning home every weekend to see Mum and to help in any way that I could. These times were very special, not least because I had heard from some Christian friends in Aberystwyth that there was a flourishing church just three miles from home, in Letterston. I went to see the vicar, the Revd Bill Lewis and his wife, Chloris. They really took me under their wing and as a 'babe in Christ' and a recent convert, this was a great blessing. They taught me a huge amount about my new life in Christ. This church, under Bill's leadership, was growing quite fast. It was strongly influenced by the 'charismatic movement' which grew rapidly in the UK during the mid to late 1960s. Our friends Christine and Catherine had also been converted as a result of this movement. A little later, it impacted some other churches in the Church in Wales. I believe that my new faith came about indirectly from this new movement of the Holy Spirit.

I attended Mathry church with Mum on Sunday mornings and Letterston church in the evenings. It was an interesting experience. Some good friends from the university (with whom

I travelled home) were also from Letterston. They went to Saron Baptist chapel. This Welsh Baptist chapel was also Spirit-led and evangelical, and there was a wonderful spirit of unity between the church and the chapel, with a number of shared services. This was as unusual then as it is now.

The years 1974 to 1976 provided a good grounding for me in my Christian walk in so many ways. For example, I read many books, in particular the works by Dr Martyn Lloyd-Jones and his series on St Paul's Epistle to the Romans. I read his book, *Atonement and Justification* several times.[1] It was wonderful to truly get to grips with the doctrine of 'justification by faith alone,' as experienced by Martin Luther, John Wesley, and other great Christian people. Dr Lloyd-Jones came to preach in Aberystwyth around 1975. It was lovely to hear his expository preaching, an experience I shall never forget. We also had a Bible study group in the place where I worked and they were helpful. I had a thorough grounding in the Christian faith, at first almost exclusively in the conservative evangelical tradition. The charismatic element entered the scene slightly later, giving me a good experience of both. God seemed to be exposing me to a rich tapestry of different Christian traditions, and in retrospect, I believe that this was specific training by God as a key preparation for future work with those from other denominations.

At that time my experience was further enriched by spending a week near Llandudno at Tŷ'r Brodyr, an Anglican Franciscan Friary. I also spent a week visiting St Michael-le-Belfry church in York, a major spiritual hub for the UK charismatic movement, where the Revd David Watson was the vicar. There were great similarities between the friary and St Michael's, for example in that of unconditional love freely given. I was able to see God working

1. Martyn Lloyd-Jones, *Romans: An Exposition of Chapters 3:20–4:25: Atonement and Justification*. The Banner of Truth Trust, 1970.

through the richness of the variety of his church. Another variety was in the type of people who were Christians. Although I mainly moved within the academic world, many, of course, did not. For example, I had great fellowship with a Pentecostal lady named Martha who was the WPBS cook and became a good friend. Also, there were a number of distinguished scientists within my larger group. Who said that science or a related discipline is contradictory to Christianity? The university's two leading mathematicians were Christians; Professor John Heading, the head of the department, and Professor Ken Walters (later to be elected as a fellow of the Royal Society). The former was a member of the Plymouth Brethren, the latter, a leader in charismatic circles. Yet we all had that 'oneness in Christ' and we learned a lot from each other's traditions, theology, and experience.

I didn't have the time, and no longer felt the call, to become a lay reader. However, I continued taking part in services in Mathry, and I still kept in touch with the Archdeacon of St Davids, who had become a friend. In 1975 I was surprised to receive a telephone call from him to ask whether I would be willing to be considered as a member of the (Anglican) Church in Wales' Governing Body (GB). There are six dioceses in the principality and a rule had just been passed that two from each diocese under the age of thirty should be co-opted. Well, I was twenty-five. They had already appointed one person from my diocese, an ordinand (trainee vicar) from Carmarthen. So I was honoured to be the second person from St Davids diocese to be appointed under this new system. Again, this was a further widening of my Christian experience and totally unexpected. We met for two days, twice a year. The Governing Body at that time had two hundred and fifty members, approximately one hundred and twenty-five clergy, and one hundred and twenty-five laity (non-clergy). It meant, for me, a further association with, and receipt of great ongoing kindnesses from my bishop the Rt Revd Eric Roberts, the Bishop of St Davids. Besides our meetings, we also had regular correspondence. My membership of this rather august body lasted for six years, as I was re-elected by our diocese after my first three years of co-option.

Again, I could see God's hand at work in widening my Christian experience. Perhaps the majority of the clergy in the Church in Wales were Anglo-Catholic in theology, but there were also a few of us of evangelical belief, a misused term but by which I mean quite simply accepting the authority of the Bible in all matters of faith and doctrine, rather than adding on human tradition as of equal authority. There were two people I came to know over this period who were particularly special, and who opened my eyes to see God working through other traditions. One was the mother superior of an Anglican convent within the St Davids diocese. She was a very great Christian lady of deep spirituality.

The other was the Rt. Revd. John Poole-Hughes, the then assistant bishop of Llandaff. He had previously been a missionary and became the Bishop of SW Tanganyika (now Tanzania), but had felt it right to give up his position to make way for an African bishop and so he returned to Wales, his homeland. I had a lovely chat with him about my conversion experience. He said, 'I am very glad to hear it! Do you mean that you have the living Christ within?' My answer was a definitive yes! I asked him respectfully about his take on confirmation in Scripture, in the light of earlier baptism. He replied that it was a quite normal experience, and frequently happened, that whenever he confirmed believers in Africa, they were filled with the Holy Spirit on this special occasion. It was wonderful to hear that, and I didn't know that this happened to some people. What did these people I have mentioned have in common, that felt so Christian? First, a full acceptance of the authority of the Bible and all that it teaches; second, a real openness to God and to his working. Thirdly, they had a genuine humility before the living God and a determination to be obedient to God's calling upon their lives. To me, that is an outstanding Christian.

Another organisation that was a rich blessing to so many of us in the mainstream churches around that time was the Fountain Trust. This was an ecumenical agency formed in the UK in 1964 to promote charismatic renewal. I attended an excellent conference in Aberystwyth in 1976 which they organised, and another in Westminster Central Hall, London, in 1977, which was very special. Here, at this biennial international conference, there were three thousand participants, with many Roman Catholic young people who were 'born again' and Spirit-filled. That was a real eye-opener for me given my very different tradition. Also particularly special was the range of speakers. For example, at several key sessions, two speakers shared the same platform: the Revd Tom Smail, a former Presbyterian minister, later a Church of England vicar; and Cardinal Joseph Suenens, the Archbishop of Mechelen, Brussels, Belgium, and one of the four moderators of the Second Vatican Council. Yet, we were truly one in the Spirit. I learned through these different experiences that God has his own from every Christian denomination and that he cannot be 'pigeon-holed', which as human beings we seem to rather enjoy doing.

The Revd Bill Lewis had previously explained that a prophecy had been given at a particular meeting for the Church in Wales, along the lines that the Holy Spirit would descend upon west Wales, just like the rain which comes in from the west. This was in the early 1970s, and shortly after that time there came wonderful spiritual renewal to some major Anglican churches such as Cardigan, Aberaeron, Lampeter, Tregaron, Aberystwyth, and with its continuation in Bill's church, Letterston. This was an evangelical charismatic movement of the Holy Spirit, with immense life-changing benefits for many hundreds of people. This was very different from the 1950s, when only one evangelical Anglican Church existed in Wales, on the Lleyn Peninsula. Thankfully, God acted in a sovereign way in response to the prayers of many and did a wonderful work.

Chapter Seven
God the Matchmaker!

I was pleased to be awarded my PhD in August 1976. This was the culmination of four years' work, an extra year needed because of a severe drought in 1975 and 1976. We needed to ensure that our research findings held true under very dry conditions. Thankfully, this proved to be the case. This was the end of a happy era for me.

I then moved to Reading University, where there was a vacancy for post-doctoral research along similar lines to my Aberystwyth work. This was a three-year post in their department of agricultural botany, to work on 'factors which determine grain number and yield in spring barley.' Again, this was on the whole an enjoyable experience. I loved the work and it was a fruitful time for me from an academic perspective, not least with some interesting findings concerning apical dominance and its manipulation in both barley and other cereal crops which had practical applications.

It was during this time that God became my matchmaker! Being a Christian in those days meant that you needed to have quite serious intentions before asking a girl out. At least, it seemed like that, even though it wasn't actually spelt out. This is how God led me to meet my future wife. It was a three-year operation by God and I nearly blew it!

Before telling this story, I wish to make an important point concerning God's dealings with human beings. In my own life I have messed up in many ways, this is the human condition. Many or even most people have especially messed up in the area of relationships. Therefore what I am about to relate may be difficult or hurtful for some. I think the key point is that throughout this story of my own Christian life there is the thread called 'grace'. God knows our fragility but still loves each one of us completely. Some of us may have spent our whole life in messed-up human relationships, for many complex reasons, not least relating to our childhood. So if you have had five husbands or wives or whatever, or if your life has gone badly, or you are in the ditch, God will be the last person to condemn you (see John 4:18). God is always in the business of 'a fresh start'.

George Verwer, in his excellent book *Messiology*, writes along the lines that we may well have missed God's 'Plan A', but maybe we can join him for his 'Plan M', or even 'Z'.[1] That is, God wishes to pick us up wherever we are, make us his own and re-create us. These stories are all about God's goodness and leading, not about our success, works or goodness. In chapter fifteen I explain how God's answer is freely available to us.

I initially worshipped at Greyfriars Church in Reading. It was a large congregation with a substantial ministry to students and also supported several overseas missionaries – a novel concept for me. On my first Sunday, there was a student lunch at which I started talking to a lovely girl called Linda. Actually, I fell hopelessly in love with her after only five seconds! It was a mixture of her beauty and her loving-kindness which had me hooked. She had also been a student at Aberystwyth, and we had some mutual friends. She was a graduate in librarianship and English literature. Somehow, due to the large size of the congregation, I only saw her every couple of weeks. I remember sitting next to her at some church event and asking if she would like a lift home. We then had a decent chat,

1. George Verwer, *Messiology*. Moody Publishers, 2016.

and I learned more about her. In those days I had a few irrational hang-ups which now seem quite absurd. One of these was being rather in awe of those who have studied at Oxford or Cambridge University. During our chat, Linda revealed that her brother had studied at Cambridge University. It was this that meant – with my particular emotional hang-up – that I couldn't invite her out and this caused me great grief. It was a totally stupid reaction, but don't many of us have a few irrational thoughts and feelings if we are being totally honest?

After a few months, much as I appreciated Greyfriars, I started looking for a smaller, more intimate, Anglican church in Reading. I found the ideal place, St John's and St Stephen's. It was evangelical, with a focus on 'church as a spiritual family'. I loved it and became happily involved, together with other single as well as married couples. A new person called Chris joined our smallish congregation. He was starting his teaching career in music at a Reading school. We became good friends and shared a house in Reading, together with our friend Brian.

After around a year, our mutual friend Jenny invited Chris, me, and a number of others to lunch. There I met Linda once again! It was lovely to meet up with her. I asked her, in as nonchalant a manner as possible, whether she was planning to live in Reading for much longer, to which she replied that she was about to have a job interview on the Isle of Wight. I was rather gutted and prayed most earnestly that she wouldn't get the job (I think it also showed that God has a good sense of humour!).

Shortly after, I asked Chris (by now I felt like I needed to take a course in nonchalance) whether Linda had got the job, to which he replied 'no'. What I hadn't realised before this lunch was that Linda was actually Chris's sister, which had never dawned on me. I wrote to Linda at her place of work to invite her out on a date.

She kindly accepted, and we got on really well. We were engaged after several months and were married eighteen months after our second meeting.

This is the miracle that only God could do, and which totally convinces me that God is a matchmaker (not always, perhaps, but certainly in my case). In September 1976 I meet this stunningly beautiful girl who I fall hopelessly in love with, the Lord then directed me to another church where, unbeknown to me, her brother Chris and I became best friends, sharing a house together. We were married fairly soon after our second meeting, in November 1980. No obstacle is too difficult for God to overcome. By the way, we lived happily ever after as well! On a purely mathematical level, maybe a statistician, given the correct data, could calculate the probability of these several 'random' events occurring by chance. With all these events happening in sequence, I think that the probability would be well under one in several hundred. It was quite extraordinary, and I have always known that Linda has been the right girl and soul mate for me, a wonderful grace in my life.

Chapter Eight
Desert

After our wedding in 1980 and the conclusion of my post-doctoral research in Reading, I obtained a job in the plant technical field in the south of England. This move was initially enjoyable for us both and we had a very happy two years. Unfortunately, things started to go wrong at my place of work. We began to experience dishonesty at a high level with the falsification of some plant trials results which made my own position untenable. Out of integrity, I had to make a polite exit fairly quickly, much to my own and Linda's grief. This necessitated an early move, and I was grateful to obtain a job in technical sales, based near Reading.

We returned to Reading and worshipped at a very fine independent evangelical church, planted on a new estate, called Southcote Church. Here we put down good new roots and made many new friends. In this job, my new colleagues were really helpful and I received excellent training in technical sales. They taught me very well, and here I would like to single out my manager who put my colleagues and me through a lot of training which was really helpful. It was a pleasant experience in so many ways and I learned a lot about sales, dealing with customers, and working a patch (mine was three counties). It was a joy to have such excellent colleagues, many of whom I have kept in touch with over the years.

But deep down, I knew that I was 'off-track' with regard to what God had both called and trained me to do. My heart was really in agricultural research, along the lines of my ten previous happy years in research work at university. I yearned to get back into the plant research area, and I started looking for a job in my field. This wasn't at all easy as there weren't many of these jobs around. As seemed to be my lot in life, I had taken the more difficult route.

Somehow, I had to hang on to the thought that God was in all this, and perhaps was even taking the lead; though humanly speaking, things had gone pear-shaped. I also felt bad for the sake of Linda and for our little boy. During this 'desert' time we actually had five house moves in as many years; several as short-term rentals. I really didn't feel at all good about myself, even though the events that triggered all this were solely the fault of a third party. I think the recurring thought was *what a huge mistake I've made*, and *what a fool I've been*. We are often far too hard on ourselves. Sometimes difficult events occur in everyone's life. Often we need to stand back, make an honest assessment, have the courage to put the past behind us, and move on in our lives. If we trust in God, then he is ultimately in control, he will overrule our waywardness, and lead us in our next steps. If we believe in an all-powerful God who knows everything, then it is inconceivable that anything takes him by surprise.

I was also learning that there is no difference between the sacred and the secular in the Christian life. All Christian believers are equal in that respect. Whatever path God leads us into is his sacred calling and plan for our lives. For example, agricultural research, sales, housework, looking after a relative, or any other kind of honourable work, is just as important to God as becoming a vicar in the Anglican Church, or any other Christian ministry. I firmly believe that every Christian has a special calling from God. If we want God's will for our lives, then it is very important to know that God will guide us on that path.

> For we are God's handiwork, created in Christ Jesus to do good works, which God prepared in advance for us to do.
>
> (Ephesians 2:10)

What is the passion of our hearts? What good thing(s) do we really enjoy doing? What gives us fulfilment in life? These and other questions will give us assurance in following that journey of discovery in our Christian calling.

After quite a long time (about two years), I read of a vacant research post based near Colchester, Essex, with a seed company in the small town of Witham, which had an excellent research department in the nearby village of Kelvedon. It specialised in producing seed from flowers, vegetables, and agricultural crops, where the harvest period is over several months. It was based there because this is the driest part of the UK, enabling the harvesting of many crops on a continuous basis from June to October.

The company had a vacancy for a novel crops specialist, to work on new plant sources of gamma-linolenic acid (GLA), a natural precursor of prostaglandins, used for the treatment of various human conditions, including certain diseases of the immune system, eczema, and pre-menstrual tension. Oil of evening primrose is the most widely used crop source for this. The job seemed a perfect fit for me. The salary wasn't great, but it felt right and Linda also felt the same.

I applied for and, thankfully, was accepted for the job. So in September 1984 Linda, our son (now two), and I moved to Colchester and bought a small house there. I remember Linda saying, 'I think that God wants us to buy this house,' which was my exact thought as well! It just seemed that God was moving fast and slotting everything into place quickly. After our turbulent few years entailing five house moves, we just needed a place in which to settle, put down new roots and rebuild our lives. On our second Sunday in Colchester, we followed a friend's recommendation to attend St John's Anglican Church in Colchester. We received a very warm welcome from the vicar the Revd Brian Nicholson and his wife, Hilary.

Chapter Nine
Restoration

It was a great joy for Linda and me to settle down in Colchester. We felt that we had really come home after a long sojourn in the wilderness. Also, we felt that this would be for many years. To date, it has been nearly forty years and we are still here. We settled down very happily in our lovely little house in Churnwood Road. I really loved my new job. In several ways, the Holy Spirit of God reassured us that this was his will for us. The initial GLA project lasted for around two years, and I then continued at the research station working on other crops of use to the company. I researched potential new varieties of linseed, field beans, and oilseed rape. It was a time of great joy and fulfilment in my work. I felt that I had been born for this!

Of particular interest to me were our field bean varieties which were mainly bred by the state organisation of (the then) East Germany and our linseed which mainly originated from a similar setup in Hungary, so this was my first experience of dealing with the Warsaw Pact countries (a mutual defence organisation originally composed of the former Soviet Union and Eastern Europe). During the 1980s, our main method of communication with them was via telex. We received annual visits from the East German contingent during those interesting times. It was always high-level officials who visited, with two large, black, bullet-proof vehicles plus their entourage. It was rather amusing for me in many respects because a major purpose of their visit was to see my humble field bean trials!

In May 1987, I went on my first visit to a Warsaw Pact country; to Poland, for the International Rapeseed Congress, held in the city of Poznan. It was a fascinating experience to see a 'closed' Communist country. After flying to Warsaw, I took the train to Poznan, a cross-country journey that took several hours. A second-class ticket was the equivalent (in *zlotys*, the Polish currency) of 10p, with first-class at 30p. After some careful deliberation about the best use of company resources, I opted for first class. It was a great experience; not least the punctuality of the train (to the minute) and its cleanliness, plus fascinating views of Poland's agriculture in that historic era. The conference was enjoyable, and upon my return to Warsaw, I decided to do some shopping; not least to use up my zlotys which could only be spent inside the country. There was little at that time in the shops; most were empty. There was a large queue outside one, which was a toy shop, and it had just received a small supply of electronic items. I decided to avoid that, as these lovely Polish people had so few nice things to enjoy. I saw a Monopoly board (Polish version) for 30p. I wish now that I had bought it. I bought two little teddy bears for our children (which they appropriately named 'Zloty'), then I flew home.

I am convinced, in retrospect, that these early Communist-era experiences were from God, as a taste of what, unbeknown to me, would shortly take up a large portion of my life.

Meanwhile, Linda and I became involved with St John's Church. It was a time of rapid growth for the church because of the high quality of the teaching, its focus on prayer, and its outward-looking vision. We belonged to a house group led by the Revd Margaret Costorphine, a wise and humorous lady who was our curate and who helped us a lot with her counsel.

The following were some highlights of our early days:

A particular parish weekend in Sizewell, Suffolk, next to the nuclear power station, in 1986. We were asked to divide into groups, and then provide feedback to the church on our thoughts and vision for different church ministries for the next five years. Our little group focused on overseas missions and consisted of Florence, David, Celia, Linda, and myself. Florence had a prophetic message: 'Why not pray for a church member to be called out from our church to serve God overseas?' This sounded wonderful and totally surprised everyone. Nobody had thought of that before! We fed this message back to the church and this was greeted with loud acclamation. This set the scene for a significant breakthrough in the overseas mission life of our church.

We had another weekend, this time in Colchester. David Smith, an elder from St Michael-le-Belfry church, York, came to speak. I went to see him because I was still having these persistent anxiety issues. He kindly prayed over me and God gave him a prophetic word, which I have held on to ever since: 'I have loved you with an everlasting love and my love will reach the very depths of your being. Do not doubt my love, for no man can take this from you.' This is a précis of some of the words from Jeremiah 31:3 but in a different context. Those words encouraged me. Often in life, God may give Christians a verse or 'word' of hope that we can hang on to until it is fulfilled. That happened to me in this case.

A little later, under Brian's leadership, a healing ministry was introduced. This is thoroughly Scriptural and it was a blessing to see people coming up for healing prayer, and then hearing of physical and emotional healings. I decided to do the same. I was really helped by several people who kindly prayed for my emotional healing. In my case, the problem was the separation from my mother on the date of my birth for many months due to her becoming very ill and with a subsequent lack of childhood bonding. This 'separation anxiety' was tackled head-on. The key people who helped me through this inner healing process were the Revd Glanville and Hazel Martin. They lived in Alresford, near Colchester, and I visited them for healing prayer over a period of three years. I am so grateful for this and for the help that I was given. So much emotional baggage was unravelled, and I thoroughly recommend this approach to anyone suffering in this way. I thank God for this provision. As I write this book, however, I will say that I still struggle with anxiety problems, which come under the heading of 'Generalised Anxiety Disorder' (GAD). It is just 'one of those things' cards with which I have been dealt. I felt, however, that God had, in that earlier healing, greatly strengthened me for the next phases of my life.

The church's congregation was expanding significantly at this stage, to the extent that we needed a much larger building. This was a very exciting time to be at St John's. The whole building project took three years from start to finish, and it was a vast undertaking for a medium-sized congregation in a far from affluent area (by UK standards). We needed to raise around £650,000; a lot of money in those days, yet there were only around sixty to seventy wage earners in the congregation. The human arithmetic didn't look too good for a successful outcome.

The key element was the prayer part. For three years we prayed on Monday mornings, Wednesday lunchtimes, and Friday evenings. I chose Monday mornings at 7.00 am, in the caravan! We just prayed for the money to come in and many practical building matters, as many human obstacles suddenly appeared and we just prayed through each one. All giving was confidential, so that the glory would be given to God. The whole project was a tremendous faith-building exercise for our church members. We received several hundred answers to very specific prayers, and these were faithfully recorded in several diaries. The money came in fairly quickly, and we saw numerous answers to prayer on the practical building aspects. Here is an excellent account of the building project, kindly written by Liz Berry who, with her husband, Tony, and their family, lived through this time and still continue as faithful members of St John's church.[1]

OUR MIRACULOUS CHURCH BUILDING

Very early on we had some prayer in the old church vestry and were asking God how we might raise such a huge amount of money with the few people we had. Peter Holden had a specific word from the Lord saying, 'I will provide the finances like manna.' It was a very key encouragement and confirmed that we were to start (not knowing if we could finish) but to believe that as we needed God's provision it would be there – and it was.

Many times during the project we were living on the edge. We had to acquire a piece of land that belonged to a house that joined our churchyard. The people who lived there had no time or interest in the church (although Tony had known them for many years and was visiting them from time to time), but God opened their hearts to allow us to acquire it. Without this land, we couldn't have gone ahead. We had to have it for sufficient parking before planning permission was granted to build.

In the 1987 great storm (the one in which Michael Fish made his unfortunate prediction or lack of it!) a very large tree was uprooted. It had a preservation order on it and was not allowed to be touched. It was totally in the way of the new build. What a miracle! None of the other trees were blown down, only the one which was needed for us to fulfil God's plans.

When we met and prayed together, we were given the same verses of Scripture several times. One was from the book of Chronicles

1. Elizabeth Berry, personal communication.

(2 Chronicles 7:14–15), which was very much about humbling ourselves and about God 'healing the land'. Even visiting speakers or those who had no clue as to what was going on still quoted it. On the day that the cornerstone was laid, another church had a massive collection for us. They presented us with a cheque which we think was for £7,500 – but what was extraordinary was that the amount given was the exact amount of money that was needed to proceed to the next stage. God was showing himself once again to be the divine accountant!

On the day that the builders (Sadler's of Ipswich) wanted to lay the foundations, they said that it must not rain, or their work would be ruined. That morning the weather was awful – rain, cloud, etc., yet these massive trucks with concrete mixers were scheduled to arrive on that day. We prayed throughout, they arrived, laid it all in the dry and with no rain. Outside that area, however (at the roundabout by The Rover's Tye pub in Colchester and beyond) it was pouring with rain and the same happened in the other direction (by Plains Farm Close in Colchester and beyond) where it also rained hard. It was as if God had placed a large umbrella over the church.

During the early stages of the building work, there was a national brick strike. All the builders had to down tools and stop work. The site manager came into the caravan where we were praying and said that it was impossible to get bricks anywhere in the country, so they would have to stop work. We prayed for God to provide for us. The next day two lorry loads of bricks arrived on the site and so the bricklayers were able to carry on building. Even the sceptical, 'non-believing' builders thought that it was a miracle!

Alongside the building project, God was doing an even deeper work in his people. We had started the journey by faith and God was increasing it as we offered our gifts, time, and prayers to him. A very important lesson we learned was that, though there were a few 'monied' people who could easily give, the majority of us didn't have that luxury.

Therefore we had to be creative and ask God to show us what we could do to release finance. It was a vital principle to learn as it kept the family of God together, knowing that we could all be involved at some level.

A key person was Eric Honeyball, who was the building treasurer. Even if just a few coins came in he was so thankful and praised God for it. There was something about thankfulness and gratefulness that we needed to understand. The children in the Sunday School would give a few pence from their pocket money, a lady would offer to do the ironing for someone, and other people would bake cakes to sell, do some cleaning or gardening and put the money received into the building fund. It was a way of understanding that we all had gifts that we could use to the glory of God and felt so much part of the whole family's giving. Praying in the caravan was very exciting, so much so that if you couldn't make a prayer session, people would phone someone to ask what God was saying or doing and how we should pray next. We understood that it was costly to give our time sacrificially, but so rewarding.

Personally, many times when we gave financially we struggled a bit because we had needs at home and for our family, but God graciously provided all that we needed as a family and more! I can remember when our stair carpet became threadbare and almost dangerous. There was a Gift Day and we gave away the money which I'd hoped would provide us with a new carpet. I wrestled with that but we gave it anyway. A couple of days later a friend called round and said he was fitting new carpets into a 'posh' house and had been asked to rip out carpets that he said: 'had nothing wrong with them.' He said that there would be enough for our hall, stairs and landing and he could fit them for us for £25, a small percentage of what we'd given away and we'd never have been able to afford such a high-quality wool carpet.

We had many questions, doubts and fears about God's provision for us when we started on this journey. However, what we learned through it couldn't have happened in any other way. We ended by saying 'Jehovah

> Jireh', the Lord is our provider! We saw that the figures didn't add up. It had to be God doing the multiplication. We understood much more about having faith – believing for what we cannot yet see (Hebrews 11:6). We recognised that it couldn't work unless we all did our little bit, and understood more about thankfulness and our dependency on God. Our lives were changed by the living God in whom we had put our trust.

I will never forget our last Giving Day in the church. It was on a Saturday, and I saw a 'holy presence' by the holy table in the new church. It was continuously there, and I was slightly frightened by this. Apparently, a number of people saw this, and it was an angel. Words fail me. By the grace of God, we raised the £650,000, the sum finally needed to pay for the building and in fact, we had around £12,000 left over. Many of those praying felt that this money should be made as a gift to others who had a similar project. This was fulfilled a little later, on behalf of Moldova and Romania, which I will explain in chapter thirteen.

I think, as Liz explained, that the greatest gift of all was the effect on our faith and the realisation that God really does answer prayer. This stood our church in good stead for its future growth and in the lives of all who participated in this miraculous endeavour. Looking back, how could we ever doubt the living God and what he can do for his church, provided that we take the trouble to pray? God says in the Scriptures that nothing will be impossible with him (Luke 1:37).

Chapter Ten
St John's Church's Overseas Mission

In 1987 Linda and I set up a prayer group within St John's Church, under the wise authority of our vicar Brian and his wife, Hilary. We met in our house each month and it was called the World Interest Group. Numbers attending ranged from three to fourteen. A key member was Florence, the great lady who was given the original prophetic message that we should pray for one family from our church to be called out to work overseas as missionaries.

Our other major purpose was to connect with the Christian missionary organisation called Open Doors, led by a Dutchman called Brother Andrew, which at that time was praying for the downfall of Communism (there were 1,800 other prayer groups in several countries, of which we were one). We also prayed for the work of Tear Fund, a Christian relief charity, and for CMJ, the Church's Ministry amongst the Jews. This prayer group was highly significant both for Linda and me as well as for our church. We found out by sheer experience that when we pray in accordance with God's will, with specific intention and perseverance, then God will answer.

Actually, God answered in a far more powerful way than we ever thought possible. One major outcome; God called out not just one, but two families to overseas mission in the spring of 1992, after five years of monthly prayer. Thus was founded our church's overseas missions work; called the Antioch Ministry. By the grace of God and with a great team that included Viv Whitfield, an experienced missionary who had served in Peru, I led this work for its first twenty-one years.

All Christian work is a spiritual battle; a war between God and the forces of evil. I experienced this in a personal way at that time, having two car accidents. On the day that Rob and Sue, our first missionaries, were due to receive their first induction in our church, I was driving my car in Colchester when a large lorry hurtled into the back of me, causing both damage to the car and whiplash to me. Six weeks later, on the date of Tim and Ruth's induction, a similar thing happened; my car was parked outside my office and a young person, a recently qualified driver, accidentally smashed into the car. I wasn't at all surprised. So it has been throughout my and others' experience; that when God enables us to do things for him, we anger the devil and the forces of evil, resulting in attacks upon ourselves, and our families amongst others. This is never a cosy, comfortable life, but real warfare in the spiritual realm.[1]

Our church members have so far served long-term in or on behalf of the following countries: Brazil, Cambodia, China, France, Indonesia, the Middle East, Peru/Latin America, Russia, Sudan, Southern Sudan, and Thailand. For example, Tim and Ruth, one of our first church missionaries, called to serve in 1992 in the Middle East, worked tirelessly for some nineteen years. Another couple, Mark and Shirley, have worked for the Overseas Missionary Fellowship (OMF) in Cambodia; Sue has done great work in Thailand on behalf of relationally broken people; Russell and Katharine have worked

1. For more about spiritual warfare, see:

C. S. Lewis, *The Screwtape Letters: Letters from a Senior to a Junior Devil.* Collins, 2002, reprint edition.

Derek Prince, *Spiritual Warfare.* Whitaker House, USA, 2001.

Derek Prince, *Spiritual Warfare for the End Times: How to Defeat the Enemy.* Chosen Books, 2017.

in the Sudan and Nigeria on behalf of Wycliffe Bible Translators/SIL; Hugh has served in China on behalf of unreached peoples, and Laura has served in France on behalf of young people. There are others who have served with great distinction, or who are in the process of being called to serve God overseas. We came from a position of nil to seven full-time, long-term missionaries in a relatively short time. That was way beyond our original intention and we thank God for doing such wonderful work as the result of ongoing prayers by our church.

At one time we had nine members serving God overseas (around one-third from the Chelmsford diocese, the largest Episcopal area in England). At present, we have seven. Under the authority and visionary leadership of our current vicar, the Revd Andy Sachs, we now have a new church-led focus for this work, which I wholeheartedly support. Our church's vision is for fifteen long-term church members to serve God overseas, and for half the church to go on short-term overseas mission visits. Currently, we have church teams going on regular short-term mission visits to Romania under a long-term partnership led by Nik, one of our church leaders. May God bless and prosper this bold aim.

Chapter Eleven
The Fall of Communism

As we continued to pray (with other prayer groups) month by month, we saw dramatic answers to specific prayers for the release of Christian prisoners in Russia. As we continued to pray for the walls of Communism to be broken down, we witnessed the total dismantling of these political structures in the countries of Central and Eastern Europe, a 'domino effect' starting with Poland in August 1989 with the election of the first non-Communist prime minister, some ten years after the birth of the Solidarity movement. This was followed in short order by Hungary, East Germany, Czechoslovakia, Romania, and Bulgaria. Perhaps the greatest symbolic event came on 9 November 1989 when the Berlin Wall was taken down. This event was watched by many millions on TV.

The Wall was the physical expression of the Iron Curtain, built in 1961. It epitomised the division of Europe over many years. Its fall signified the end of the Cold War. Something equally dramatic, but perhaps less iconic, occurred on Christmas Day 1989: the execution of the president of Romania, Nicolae Ceauşescu and his wife, Elena. Romania was the only country in that region to have suffered any significant violence in this 'peaceful revolution'.

The many prayer groups organised by the Open Doors mission, including the one we were part of, continued praying throughout 1990 and 1991, while Russia and the Eastern parts of the former Soviet Union regimes were still intact. Mikhail Gorbachev, the president of the Soviet Union, after his election in 1985, had introduced two new policies, namely *perestroika* (restructuring) and *glasnost* (openness). Gorbachev also made it clear that Soviet military intervention in support of Communist regimes (the Brezhnev Doctrine) would be abandoned.

These changes prepared the way for what would happen in Central and Eastern Europe and, later, in other parts of the Soviet bloc, including Russia. An unsuccessful Soviet coup against Gorbachev in August 1991 finally resolved the destiny of the Soviet Union. A few days later, Ukraine and Belarus declared their independence from the Soviet Union, whilst the Baltic States sought international recognition. In December 1991, Boris Yeltsin, the new Soviet president, met with the leaders of the Ukraine and Belarus to form the Commonwealth of Independent States (CIS), which spelt the end of the Soviet Union. On 25 December 1991, the Soviet hammer and sickle flag was lowered for the last time over the Kremlin Palace in Moscow and was replaced by the Russian tricolour. With President Yeltsin now in charge of a newly independent Russian state, again it was amazing to see a relatively peaceful transition from the giant, autocratic, Communist Soviet empire (founded on 8 November 1917) into a number of newly independent states, analogous to what occurred in Eastern Europe some two years before.

Diplomatic relations were restored between the USA and Russia, Ukraine, Belarus, Kazakhstan, Armenia, and Kyrgyzstan. In February 1992, diplomatic relations were restored with other newly independent republics: Uzbekistan, Moldova, Azerbaijan, Turkmenistan, and Tajikistan. In May, diplomatic relations were restored with Georgia. Thus was overthrown more than seventy years of Soviet Communism: from the Bolshevik October Revolution in 1917 until December 1991. It was a very dark and miserable period in human history that had as part of its aim the official abolition of

Christianity across a vast expanse of the world. A flawed ideology and a failed experiment had, finally, come to an end in those states.

But this outcome was not known to us as we (and many others) started praying in 1987. All we could see at that time was the miraculous release of prisoners held for many years in Soviet prisons and the appearance of Mr Gorbachev as the Soviet president who seemed slightly different from his predecessors. Some commentators say that Mr Gorbachev's flaw was that he believed Communism could be reformed.

I would like to list a few things which God put in the mind of our small prayer group. One significant event was the opening up of the Russian postal service in 1988, which allowed Bibles to be sent directly to their recipients. Linda and I bought four hundred Jiffy bags and obtained four hundred Russian Bibles from Open Doors. We obtained contact addresses from a Swiss organisation. We contacted other churches in Colchester. I remember that Eld Lane Baptist Church in Colchester bought a hundred Bibles from us and we sold a hundred on a stall in St John's. Other churches took part, as did many individuals. We bought a very large map of the USSR, put it in our conservatory, and obtained coloured pins which we stuck into the places where the Bibles were being sent to. What we didn't expect was that we would receive moving 'thank you' letters from around 20 per cent of the recipients. Bibles were very rare in this Communist country – they were considered to be great treasures. Caroline, a member of St John's church, is a fluent Russian speaker, so we gratefully read these wonderful replies. It was quite an event, as they replied from all over Russia and Siberia, including from some very remote places. A few Bibles didn't make it and were returned by the customs offices. I think that we were greatly affected by all this, not least that we were participating in a major historical event.

Another event was the planning by our group of a Russian meal in St John's, where the invited speaker was the UK director of Open Doors, the Revd Tom Wright. This was held in February 1989 and ninety-three people came to the meal. Margaret Costorphine, our excellent curate, didn't know what the colour scheme for the meal should be for the flowers, table cloth, etc. She asked us to pray. The following morning I prayed about this in our sitting room, then went and had breakfast in the kitchen. While just standing preparing my breakfast, I heard an audible 'human' voice simply say to me 'The Lord's colours are red and gold'.

I was astounded to hear the voice of God like that in an audible way: it was a great encouragement and is rare in the Christian experience. I quickly realised that the hammer and sickle Soviet flag was also red and gold and that God's colours are red (for the blood of Jesus shed for our sins) and gold (for Jesus's kingship). So, I had been spoken to by the 'highest authority' on this matter. I quickly spoke to Margaret and so we had red and gold as our colour scheme for the Russian meal. For me, it was an awesome thing for God to speak in that way. I could never have conceived red and gold and its symbolism unless God had revealed it like that. I think too that in retrospect it was God telling me quite dramatically that I too would be 'called' in some way to serve these people.

Chapter Twelve
Romania

During the period 1987–89, the persecution of Christians in Romania under their president, Nicolae Ceauşescu, became particularly intense. I personally became very angry and disturbed about the severe injustice to believers in that country. Linda and I had already started sending food parcels to a fellow Christian in Romania. There was a UK organisation called ROMAF, the Romanian Aid Fund, and we started supporting and giving to them. This deep stirring within me continued for many months. In 1989 I went to an annual conference of theirs, the speaker was Dr Josef Tson, a Romanian pastor and theologian. He later became a friend, and I have been greatly influenced by his teaching. I had read in the ROMAF bulletin that a new organisation had been formed in the UK, the Romanian Missionary Society (RMS). RMS was already very active in the USA where their work included the much-needed preparation of theological literature into the Romanian language. Under the wise direction of Dr Josef Tson, thousands of copies of more than sixty theology textbooks had been produced and smuggled into Romania, for Christian training purposes.[1]

The purpose of the UK charity of RMS was to arrange and finance the training of pastors and theologians in secret, in preparation for the ending of Communism in that country. At one time there

1. Danut Manastireanu, 'Western Assistance in Theological Training for Romanian Evangelicals to 1989', *East–West Church Ministry Report*. Vol. 14, no. 3, summer 2006.

had been many trained pastors in Romania, but due to extreme persecution over many years the total number being trained was now limited to just a few people per year for the whole country, out of twenty-two million people. The news of this new initiative hugely appealed to me and I immediately wrote to RMS giving them as much financial help as we could and asking them how we could further help, including by prayer. Linda and I had already been writing to Christian charitable trusts on behalf of another cause and we offered to do this for them, which was graciously accepted. This innovative UK project with the vision for the training of a new generation of Romanian Christian theologians, spearheaded by Josef Tson and RMS's director Les Tidball, was put in place to enable students to study for and obtain the degrees that they needed in order to give them credibility within the Romanian education system. Les Tidball was able to make good progress through the London Bible College (LBC), now called the London School of Theology (LST), under the very able academic coordination of Dr Graham McFarlane.[2]

There were initially forty-two students (able to speak English) who were divided into seven smaller groups, meeting in different cities across Romania. Couriers smuggled theological textbooks into Romania which were then distributed to the students before their meeting with the lecturer. They then met with their Western instructor for several days, listening to lectures and discussing the topic of the course. Then during the next six weeks, the students studied the texts and wrote essays on topics arranged by the lecturer. These essays were then sent to the UK via the next lecturer. After the teacher had corrected and marked the papers, they were then returned to the students.[3] All of this needed to be done in

2. Manastireanu, 'Western Assistance in Theological Training'.

3. Manastireanu, 'Western Assistance in Theological Training'.

secret because of the severe Communist regime and to avoid any attention from the brutal secret police, the Securitate.[4] This was how theological training was done during the Communist era. It was a major logistical work, to say the least, and Les Tidball, together with his wife, Dorothy, undertook this with great ability.

During 1989 and for the following twelve years, I researched and wrote many letters to Christian trusts (often several hundred a year) on behalf of RMS, and we obtained a lot of money for the work through this approach. I was greatly helped by Florence, who prayed with me and helped me to research and write to the trusts. Also, in 1989 Les Tidball rang to say that he and Josef would like to meet up with us in Colchester. Linda and I invited them to lunch and we had a precious time together. They kindly invited me to be a member of their board and I was honoured to accept. Although our various meetings were mainly held in Torquay, we also met at the London Bible College and at several other locations. After a few months, I also became one of six trustees of RMS.

I continued working for RMS for many years; from 1989 until the work's completion in 2000. The chair of trustees was the Revd Arthur Neil, a lovely Christian man who, later in his life, had a ministry of exorcism, and God used him to free Doreen Irvine, which is recorded in her book (*From Witchcraft to Christ*), the book through which my friend Mike had been converted. As trustees, we met around five times a year, plus I did fundraising for them. It was in my spare time as I had a full-time job and it was rather onerous, but full of joy and fulfilment as well. It was most certainly part of 'God's call' for me. When I joined RMS the training had to be undertaken in secret, as explained above, due to their very oppressive regime. On Christmas Day, 1989, all of this

4. Manastireanu, 'Western Assistance in Theological Training'.
Les Tidball, personal communication.

was transformed by the Romanian revolution which saw the death of President Ceauşescu and the sudden opening up of that country. It was a tremendous freedom and many people were able to enter Romania and provide help in different ways.

RMS was now free to arrange for these theological students to be trained over here in the UK, rather than through the previous distance learning which had to be done in secret. Over several years, twenty of the forty-two Romanian students came to the UK and completed their BA or MA degrees at LBC. They then returned to Romania to continue with their ministries. Ten of these graduates also obtained their PhD degrees and then returned to Romania to teach theology in existing university faculties.[5]

God's plans had been much greater than ours. There were only a few trained pastors in 1989, many had been shot, imprisoned, had been killed by arranged car accidents, or had simply died during that awful regime. Our original intention had been to train only a few students, but the end result was the training of twenty, many with PhDs, who were then allowed to return to Romania and teach in its theological faculties. Eternity will show the fruit of this work. Romania is recognised by many as being one of the most Christian countries in Europe and I am convinced that RMS has played a significant role in this.

It is the long-term fruitfulness that is the 'acid test' of Christian endeavour; this is also true in nature as well as in God's work. It was certainly an immense privilege for me. However, with the gracious help of my co-trustees, I had learned how to run a charity. I didn't realise then that God would have a lot more in store for me. I had thought that RMS would be the limit of my involvement on behalf of the former Warsaw Pact members and its post-Communist Christian reconstruction, but I was proved wrong.

5. Manastireanu, 'Western Assistance in Theological Training'.

God spoke to me personally in two very specific ways during the late 1980s and early 1990s, and it was only afterwards that I fully realised their significance. First, I had been given a prophetic word that 'I would be called from the Far West to the Far East.' Well, I was born and brought up in the 'Far West' – only two miles from the coast in Pembrokeshire, West Wales, and Linda and I moved in 1984 to Colchester for my work, (about 120 miles away), which in my mind was most certainly the 'Far East'! I had no plans or ambitions to go further east, until the Romanian connection. The second specific word from God was in our church house group, around 1997, wisely and ably led by our dear friend Jenny Woodhouse. People were kindly praying for me one evening and one man was given a picture by God of 'a pen and a bottle of rich blue ink'. I could not understand the significance of this, particularly as it had come out of the blue. I had to leave that 'word' as it made no immediate sense and I was happy to leave this in God's hands. It was fulfilled later, in Russia, and it referred to Bible translation.

A final mention about Romania: Linda and I were, of course, absolutely thrilled by the opening up of Romania in December 1989. ROMAF very quickly sprang into action with Bible distribution and we, amongst many others in the UK, became involved. We bought a hundred Romanian Bibles and were given the Romanian addresses by ROMAF. We already had spare Jiffy bags from the Russian Bible venture. We again had a stall in St John's and quickly sold these Bibles which were immediately sent to Romania. They were, as with Russia, considered to be real treasures by the Romanian people and it was a joy to be able to assist in this small way.

Chapter Thirteen
The Republic of Moldova

Moldova is a relatively small country, about the size of Wales. It is a former Soviet republic, sandwiched between Romania and Ukraine. Maybe the only reason why some people will have heard of it is that in the mid-90s they beat Wales at football 3–2, much to the consternation of my compatriots! I would not have been involved in Moldova if I had not first been working on behalf of Romania. During my time at RMS, I visited Romania a few times and met up with Pavel who lived in the city of Suceava, in northern Romania. Later I was invited to tea by my friends Peter and Maggie in Hadleigh, Suffolk, where I once again met up with Pavel and, as was usually the case with this great man, he challenged me. He had made several visits to Moldova after it had opened up in 1991. He explained that it was a country of four million people (far fewer now, as many younger people have migrated to Romania and other parts of Europe), but it was very poor; by far the poorest country in Europe according to virtually all statistical tables.

In the poorest part of this poor country, in the south-west, in the regions of Cahul, Cantemir and Leova, there were three evangelists, Sasha, Andrei, and Zahar (Alexander, Andrew and Zechariah in English), who had started to plant churches throughout that region. Mainly, they needed a salary to do this properly on a full-time basis, plus further resourcing. Could Linda and I help? I said that we had to think and pray about this. Pavel did promise to ask others to give, as he was on a three-week visit to various parts of the UK.

Oddly, after praying and discussing this with Linda, privately I liked the idea very much; it grew on me that this would be a totally worthwhile project. When I met up with Pavel three weeks later, I asked him who else was willing to help. He said that he had asked everybody, but he had received help from nobody. Linda and I were delighted to be able to give a positive answer. In September 1993, I went to Suceava and met three men who, through their evangelistic work in Moldova, became successful pastors and effective church planters. The truth is that I loved what I heard about their work and everything about them spoke of integrity and authenticity.

This new opening for Christian service was a real joy. I shouldn't really talk about money and any giving on our part, as the Scriptures make it clear that this should be done privately. Please take it as read that in all our dealings on our journey, we did our best as stewards of God's resources. Actually, if we had held back, then I don't think that God would have continued to use us as he did. He would have used someone else, and I believe that God would have been fully justified in doing so.

There were two further incidents on this visit to Romania. First, Pavel asked me to preach that evening at a very large church meeting (Baptist) in Suceava. But I am no preacher, the event was only two hours later and I had no text! Thankfully I had prepared something before leaving home just in case, knowing that these things can be sprung upon you without notice. So, feeling very inadequate, I faced a congregation of five hundred Romanian Christian people and somehow got through my sermon with sanity just about intact. But I did say to Pavel, 'Please don't *ever* do that to me again!' The second incident was during the nine-hour drive from Suceava to Bucharest to catch my flight home.

We left after a very earnest prayer by Pavel (a bit too earnest, I thought), but there had been very heavy rain in eastern Romania, with serious flooding over a large area. About halfway through our journey, we nearly drowned. There was a very simple bridge over a large river which was totally flooded, with around twenty people standing near it, carrying their cases and all their worldly goods. Pavel, in his inimitable driving style, decided to 'go for it', and so it was that we found ourselves stationary (the car's engine had stalled), with water rapidly rising halfway up our door windows. Pavel did say 'Pray!' but I was already doing that! He tried the ignition again and, miraculously, the engine started. We quickly moved forward and, thankfully, we survived this incident.

I wanted very much to visit Moldova itself, just to get to know these three people and to understand a little more about their country. It was a big investment for Linda and me, in prayer and in other ways. The opportunity arose a year later, early in December 1994.

Our church house group, led as before by our wonderful friend Jenny, kindly prayed for me before I left. A friend was given a 'picture' from God, of me being driven in a gold carriage and being carried at speed, but in safety. That encouraged me. Before leaving, I visited a charity shop in Colchester and, very surprisingly, saw a genuine Russian fur hat. I don't think that they had ever received one before. I bought it, thinking 'this could be useful'. It cost me £2.50. I left Stansted airport on 8 December en route for Bucharest, Romania; there to be picked up by Andrei and driven to Moldova.

I had just heard that weather conditions had suddenly worsened; freezing weather, snow, and roads starting to be closed. This was unusual for early December. In fact, unbeknown to me, these weather conditions were about to become the worst for many years, with many killed on the roads where I was heading. However, we drove north from Bucharest to Iasi (about a four-hour drive), and from there across the frontier from Romania into Moldova. There were four frontier crossing points in those days, as the Soviet dismantling had not yet fully reached these parts. The wait to cross the frontier took eleven hours, in addition to the four-hour drive. We weren't prepared to pay a bribe, so they kept us waiting in the freezing cold. We got through at 8.00 am and arrived at Andrei's home by 9.30.

The frontier man at the Moldovan side was very nice. He said, 'You are the third person called Williams from England to have passed this frontier in three months. Are you related?' I thought that this was rather amusing. I knew the other two: the intrepid Stephen Williams and David Williams (also unrelated to one another), both from Birmingham. I came to know them well in future years. By lunchtime, all the roads in Eastern Romania, plus all the airports, were closed because of the worsening weather and were kept closed for a week – until just one hour before my scheduled flight back home!

I really appreciated the kind hospitality of Andrei, Lydia and their three children, plus Lydia's mother who was staying. Their life was very basic. He was the Baptist pastor in Vadul-lui-Isac, a large village of around four thousand people. The people were really poor. The previous winter, several hundred had died in their village because of malnutrition, and Andrei had to bury many of them. A hundred tonnes of maize had been distributed, but this did not provide a proper diet. The next winter and thereafter, they distributed potatoes to the very poor, which did provide sufficient nutrition to enable survival. It was minus 12 °C outside and it snowed heavily much of the time.

What can I say about my first impressions? The wonderful hospitality of Andrei, Lydia, and others stands out in my memory. They didn't have much, but they shared what they had. There was little in the shops, but they had a large garden, devoted entirely to 'vegetables and edibles'. So, everything was pickled (vegetables) or bottled (fruit) for the winter. No fridge, but lots of jars. They also had some chickens, even in winter. For visitors, it was eggs or chicken, plus bread and porridge, with semolina quite often as pudding, again almost entirely for visitors.

They had an outside toilet, which was a decent walk down their garden. I have interesting memories of walking out during the night, in minus 12 °C, to a shack with a deep hole and squatting on two planks. I got used to it and quite enjoyed it. It worked! Well, everything worked, but just a bit differently from England. This felt like a visit not just to Eastern Europe but also to the fourteenth century. My visit happened to coincide with a week of mission in Cahul. So each night we went to a large church there. It was always full, perhaps with four hundred people, many of whom were there to hear the Gospel for the first time. As a foreign visitor, I was asked to say something each evening. It was mostly a few words of greeting, but I gave my conversion testimony once or twice and spoke about 'Jesus the Good Shepherd' on another occasion.

On the Sunday I went to Vadul-lui-Isac, Andrei's church, which was really special; very warm, very poor people, and with a lovely choir. It was full each Sunday, again with around four hundred people. I felt at home there and I was asked to give a short message. I was struck by the holiness and loving-kindness of the Christians that I met. They had a very hard life with much suffering, but lots of joy as well. I really bonded that week with Andrei and his family. The cold weather also helped our bonding. I think they thought 'This guy is prepared to come and see us in winter; that is unusual and appreciated. He must love us.'

That week I also met and came to know Zahar (who kept bees and produced pure Acacia honey of the highest quality), his wife, Elena, their parents, and their five children; and Sasha, his wife, and two children. I also met a missionary from Northern Ireland, Mark McCormick. It was bitterly cold and Sasha's wife very kindly gave me a pair of their winter socks which were very effective. Very sadly, Sasha had recently become unwell. During the Soviet times, only four years previously, he was ordered to take part in an 'experiment' and had to drink aeroplane fuel in order to assess its effects on human health. Sasha developed stomach cancer because of this and sadly died in 1996.

Another memory during that visit was of Andrei driving in a heavy blizzard and seeing an elderly, stooped lady carrying twigs/branches for fuel. I also met some English teachers that week in Cahul. I had been looking for a large detailed map of Moldova to bring home, but Moldovan maps were virtually non-existent in those days. It transpired that one of the teachers had a large wall map of Moldova and she wanted my Russian hat! So we did an exchange. Zahar, Sasha, and Andrei very kindly put crosses on this map, with each cross representing a church that they had planted. There was an impressive twenty-one in total. These three men of God had done a very effective job of church planting resulting in congregations throughout southwest Moldova. What a great thing to do! I was really honoured to be involved.

We were still snowed in after a week. The roads were impassable and Bucharest airport was still closed. My plane was due to leave on the Wednesday afternoon. Amazingly, on the Tuesday, the airport was re-opened and the weather suddenly improved. Andrei and friends kindly drove me back on the Tuesday evening, travelling overnight. The snow had cleared, the frontier crossing was fairly short because of the weather, but we had to hand in our passports in one place to be checked and were asked to step out and wait. It was a long wait in minus 12 °C in the open. There was no reason for this as they weren't busy. We were the only travellers. It was another 'just because they could' experience. Eventually, we received permission to go on our way and we arrived in Bucharest by late morning. Bucharest airport was now open; I caught my flight and came home.

I thought I would spend my last Romanian *lei* on something for Linda. I saw a lovely box of Romanian chocolates – different shapes, sizes and wrappings. They looked lovely and I came home with these, plus my Moldovan map. Soon Linda and I were having our first chocolate tasting session. She went first, with something big, round and wrapped. It had a possible fruit flavour. I had something smaller, rectangular, and caramel-looking. We sampled several more and they were tasty, even interesting, but then it gradually dawned on us that all the chocolates were exactly the same flavour. They were quite nice in their own way, but they tasted identical. We had a very good laugh over our Romanian chocolate experience. These were very early post-Communist days and to have chocolates at all was a bit of a luxury.

I made three further visits to Moldova, in 1997, 1999 and 2001. These visits were primarily to share fellowship with Andrei and Lydia, Zahar and Elena, and Mark and Mari McCormick. I stayed with Andrei and Lydia on all four occasions. There are a few key things that I would like to share:

During my second visit (1997) we visited the autonomous Gagauz region of south-east Moldova (Lydia's sister is married to a Gagauz man). It was a new and interesting experience for me, as I had read about them in the reference book *Operation World* by Patrick Johnston.[1] They are a unique people group within Moldova, of Turkic origin. There are approximately 150,000 living in Moldova. They are one of only a few Christianised Turkic people

1. Patrick Johnstone, Jason Mandryk and Robyn Johnstone, *Operation World: 21st Century Edition*. Authentic Lifestyle, 2001.

groups in the world and so are of immense strategic importance for other worldwide Turkic peoples.

Operation World reported that in 1991 a revival had taken place amongst these predominantly Orthodox people, resulting in up to 4,000–10,000 new Christians. There are now several Baptist churches in that region. I found it difficult to understand my immense interest in them at that time, but I think that this was planted by God and it was only many years later that I realised why this was the case. When I got involved in Bible translation work, God helped our UK charity and myself to give them their first-ever New Testament. It was a great privilege.

Our first visit to the Gagauz took us to the village of Vulcanesti, just a short distance from the border with Ukraine. Andrei and Zahar came, in addition to myself and two other people. The Gagauz speak Russian and Gagauz, but not Romanian (the language spoken by most people in Moldova). I remember a large church gathering (Baptist), with two translators working in tandem while Andrei was preaching, one translating from Romanian to Russian for the Gagauz congregation and the other from Romanian to English for our small contingent. The service lasted for around three hours, and then we were invited to the house of Vera and her family who put on the most wonderful Gagauz meal for at least a dozen people. We received warm hospitality and fine food. The Gagauz are renowned for carpet-making amongst many other things, and I remember beautiful multi-coloured carpets hanging on their walls. But the reality was that these people were poor. They were, however, very rich in other ways. The second visit was in 1999 and this time to Congaz, where Lydia's brother-in-law lived. That was also a three-hour service, which they seemed to specialise in, in their Baptist church. As always, as a foreign person, I was asked to speak a few words of greeting.

So, these were my initial Gagauz experiences, but what a joy and blessing they were!

God did another miraculous thing, which was very humbling. This involved Mark, my missionary friend from Northern Ireland. A group of believers had been established in Gotesti through the work of Sasha and two young ladies, Larisa and Aliona. Mark had joined this group and under his leadership, this had grown into a sizeable congregation, now in need of a church building. That was in 1996. Mark's ministry was at that time mainly financed by a small charity called the European Aid Trust (EAT). The cost of a new church building would be £20,000; far too great an amount for the charity to raise. A trustees' meeting was arranged for the following week and Mark asked us all to pray. I was pleased to do this.

A couple of days later I received a call from a man living near my home village in Castlemorris, North Pembrokeshire, who was building a few new houses there. I happened to own a small vegetable patch where he was building, which my father had previously owned. It hadn't been worth anything, and I had tried to sell it a few years earlier. But now, due to a new entrance road having been built for the houses, he rather badly needed this plot! After some negotiation, we agreed on a figure of £8,000, upon which we as a family were able to add a little. I then relayed this to my friend Stephen Williams, who chaired the EAT charity. So the trustees met and agreed to build the church.

God performed a wonderful miracle at exactly the right time: to convert a small, abandoned, overgrown vegetable patch, into almost half the cost of building a church. It was a real thrill for me. It wasn't my generosity, it was God's. Two years later (in 1999), I went on a one-week mission to Moldova with Stephen and his church from Kitts Green, Birmingham. During that time, the EAT officially opened the new church building and I was asked to say a few words. My friend Jenny had received a prophetic word that I was able to share: 'Enlarge the place of your tent, stretch your tent curtains wide, do not hold back; lengthen your cords, strengthen your stakes. For you will spread out to the right and to the left.' (Isaiah 54:2–3.) It was a powerful 'word' that Mark took to heart, and we had a long discussion about it later that day.

God has been fulfilling that prophecy ever since. In fact, in 1999, the very year the building at Gotesti was opened, God converted a lady in Chircani (the village to the immediate left or west of Gotesti). This was the beginning of a church in that village which has now grown to fifteen members, and they also now have a church building. Evangelistic work has also begun in Gheltosu to the right or east and Constantinovca to the left or west, although churches have not yet been established in either village.

Here in the West, we can be rather blasé about our church buildings; perhaps thinking 'the church is the people, not the building'. That, of course, is true, but in Moldova, Romania, and other former Soviet-dominated countries, a physical building is also needed, so that the congregation can become accepted by the local people in the village as something other than a cult, especially with some fine Orthodox church buildings in the same village.

The new church building in Gotesti seemed to legitimise the church in the eyes of the villagers, and soon many people began to come to evangelistic meetings – up to two hundred at times. The building was also used for conferences, and for similar events, with churches from all around the district attending.

At the time it cost about £20,000 to construct the church building. A year or two later, inflation started to escalate in Moldova and Romania, so the cost in 2020 for such a building would be upwards of £100,000.

The third matter which I would like to highlight is as follows:

during the St John's Colchester building project in 1986–88, the church heard from God that any money left over should be given to other churches in order to help them do the same because God had been so generous in helping us to raise over £650,000 from our own resources, except for a gift of £25,000 from the Church of England. In fact, we had £12,000 left over and applications were invited from the congregation (this was in 1997). I asked my friend Stephen who was preaching extensively in Moldova and Romania, and who was in a good position to research the possibilities over there. He came up with a list of four much-needed projects: three in Moldova and one in Romania. The total costs for two new church buildings in Moldova, a large church extension in Andrei's church, and half the cost of a church in Romania (Sammy's church) came to just over £10,500.

I was invited to attend our church's Giving Group which was appointed to oversee the £12,000 gift. Also present was a great man, Roger Maggs, who had a special vision and ministry for Israel. It was the unanimous decision of the group that the £10,500 should be given for Moldova/Romania, with a 10 per cent tithe to be given for Christian ministry in Israel. It was a great decision by our church. So, from the gifts for St John's building project, we had our own excellent new building, plus a further three and a half new churches or equivalent, plus a tithe for Israel. Again, God's timing was perfect, as all buildings were completed just before inflation took off. Now such buildings would be far more expensive to build.

In 2001, I was able to travel to Moldova with our vicar from St John's, the Revd Bob Fuller and Jenny Woodhouse, plus two other good friends Leo and Elaine, to visit these churches and see the fruit of our church's giving. There had been 'people problems' with one of the churches, but the others were a great blessing to the Christian church and I am very grateful to our church for their generosity which enabled this to happen. This visit with Bob and friends was particularly special and joyful, and I was greatly blessed by Bob's encouragement and friendship.

Linda and I continued our involvement in support of Moldova until my retirement from paid work in 2013, thus being of use to them for almost exactly twenty years, even though we did not physically visit that country after 2001. I wish to add that for just under thirty years and based in Colchester, I also had a very fulfilling 'day job' in agricultural research within the field of crop physiology, latterly as the technical manager of an agricultural chemical company where the main office was based in Ghent, Belgium. I had great colleagues and between us, we made a significant contribution to cereal crop research where we were able to innovate or develop new products for increased or maintained yields in this and in other countries. This, however, is not the focus of this book, but it was nonetheless an important time work-wise for myself and my colleagues, and a very enjoyable experience.

Chapter Fourteen
Russia/CIS and the Former Soviet Union

The work on behalf of Romania was fulfilled in the year 2000 when the Romanian Missionary Society (RMS UK) completed the training of the Romanian theological students in the UK. They then returned to their country to work in its university theology faculties.

In 1997, I was listening to a sermon by Dr Josef Tson. In his sermon, he talked about the huge need for the Christian gospel to be preached amongst the unreached indigenous peoples of the former Soviet Union where there are 130–150 non-Slavic languages spoken, by some eighty-five million people. He said, 'This is now our mission field!' I had not heard about these peoples, and I had always thought of the Soviet Union as more or less a single entity, speaking just a few languages. I researched further and found in Patrick Johnstone's book *Operation World* that the Institute for Bible Translation (IBT), a specialist Bible translation organisation, was already working amongst these peoples.[1] I was aware of the impact on the Christian life of a whole nation in having the Bible in its own language, not least in my own country, with the first complete Bible translated into Welsh by Bishop William Morgan in 1588. It had a massive effect on Welsh Christianity and, through its various revivals, God used the Welsh people in a major way to

1. Johnstone, Mandryk and Johnstone, *Operation World.*

bring Christianity to other parts of the world.[2] It was a real thrill to come across IBT, and Linda and I wrote to them in 1999 with a pledge to give regular financial support to a Bible translation project. We chose the Kumyk translation project based in the mountainous Caucasus region, a Turkic language spoken by about half a million indigenous people, and were delighted to be able to help in this small way.

A year later I received an unexpected message from Stefan Rizell, IBT's International Director, asking to meet me in London. His request was 'Could you set up our IBT charity in the UK?' That was a very big request, but God had already prepared my heart for this. Not least by having served as a trustee of RMS for twelve years, I had excellent role models for my training in running a charity. I also had current contacts with some grant-making trusts for finance, the personal desire to undertake further work after the fulfilment of RMS, and my heart's deep desire to help this important and strategic cause in whatever way I could. My answer to Stefan was 'Yes, I'd be delighted!'

Stefan was based in Sweden, where the work was founded by Dr Borislav Arapović in 1973, and their International Board was based in Stockholm. However, after the post-Soviet opening up of Russia and the CIS in December 1991, a new charity was set up in Moscow itself, with official Russian registration in 1995. Stefan was very helpful and he devoted a lot of his time and energy to instruct me about this work. I spent time with him in Sweden and he spent a week with me in London. I learned a huge amount from him. It was fascinating to hear that half of their staff in Russia were Russian Orthodox by tradition, the other half being Protestant.

IBT had around two hundred staff and co-workers. They were

2. *Beibl Byw – Wales to the World*. The Union of Welsh Independents, 4 February 2016.

working in sixty translation teams throughout Russia/CIS and their main operational centre was in St Andrew's (Andreevsky) Orthodox Monastery in Moscow, which is also the location of the Synodal Library of the Russian Orthodox Church. Besides this, in 1983 IBT Finland was founded in Helsinki which specialised in Bible translation into Russia's twenty-four Finno-Ugric languages and was headed by Anita Laakso. IBT is affiliated with the nearby Russian Academy of Sciences, working under their aegis. It is also a member of the Forum of Bible Agencies International (FOBAI), working in partnership with other Bible translation agencies such as the United Bible Societies, Wycliffe Bible Translators/SIL, and Pioneer Bible Translators, with around a quarter of IBT's projects being undertaken with one or more of these partners, the other 75 per cent by IBT on its own.

IBT's new UK charity would be the ninth country to be financially involved, not many for such extensive work. The others were Russia, Sweden, Finland, Norway, Denmark, Switzerland, the USA, and the Netherlands. It took me far longer to put the charity in place than at first envisaged, probably about eighteen months. I had a terrific group of co-trustees, and particular thanks go to my friend Stephen Williams (see chapter thirteen), who was both a solicitor and church pastor. Stephen helped to make our UK charity official by drawing up the trust deed, initially completed in February 2001. Juan and Katarina Almonte, based near the then London Bible College, greatly helped with friendship, prayer, and advice over several years. Stefan, Stephen, myself, Juan, and Katarina comprised the early nucleus of our UK charity.

We met in Birmingham on a regular basis and it started functioning well. Our initial goal was to raise £4,000 a year for the work and to pray regularly for the translation projects. That was a big target for us to aim for from scratch. To demonstrate God's faithfulness to us as a new charity, our accounts show that we were able to contribute £5,533 in 2002; £8,149 in 2003; £43,348 in 2004; £69,174 in 2005; £31,000 in 2006; £30,108 in 2007; and £64,865 in 2008. By the grace of God, we have been able to continue since 2008 with similar amounts.

We wrote to many charitable trusts and a number responded, several of whom have supported the charity over many years. We were especially encouraged by a lady who unexpectedly left us a legacy of one-eighth of her house. Another wonderful and surprising gift was from a charitable trust that gives money to Christian causes from royalties received from the famous hymn 'How Great Thou Art'. One year Susan Boyle included this hymn in her Christmas album, which rose to the top of the charts. A few months later, we received an astonishing £40,000 one-off gift as a result!

Early on in our work we made a commitment to pray for, and give to, the Gagauz and Kumyk Bible translation projects. We were interested in the Gagauz people (ethnically Turkic) because several of our UK trustees had met them. We felt that it was far too much for our small new charity to suddenly begin praying for a hundred and thirty people groups. So we concentrated on just praying for these two. God really heard our prayers and encouraged us. For example, several years later, when we were in Moscow for meetings, I just 'happened' to meet up with a Kumyk translator at breakfast who was paying a very rare visit to Moscow. I am sure that this was God's 'coincidence' which most Christians seem to experience from time to time. It was God's love and provision; I found it a moving experience.

For the Gagauz, when it came to the final editing and publication of the Gagauz New Testament, we felt it right to try and raise all the funds for this, totalling £35,000. In the summer months, I wrote around two thousand letters to UK churches. We had a very good response, over £8,000, but far short of what was needed. Then that October I received an unexpected phone call from the manager of a large trust who had received an earlier letter from me. He said, 'How much more money do you need for this?' The answer was £26,600. 'We will discuss this at our meeting shortly, but I cannot promise anything.'

Three weeks later a cheque arrived in the post for £26,600. I just sat down and wept. It was a truly magnificent gift and was the answer to many prayers. The full £35,000 paid for a further five years of final editing, plus the first print run (into both Latin and Cyrillic scripts) of the New Testament in the Gagauz language. The Gagauz people, as explained, are one of only a few Christian Turks in the world, a strategic people. Some of the Gagauz travel to Turkey to evangelise there. I met one person in Moldova who was doing this on a regular basis. They don't need visas, they are culturally very similar and the Gagauz and their language can be understood by Turkish speakers. As explained, there had been a revival amongst the Gagauz around 1991. Was this God's providence due to their significance? Many Baptist churches were formed at that time amongst these predominantly Russian Orthodox people.

IBT's UK charity currently has six trustees, including two overseas missionaries to the UK: one from South Korea, the Revd Dr Guichun Jun; the other from Russia, Anton Ponomarev, who comes from the Russian Orthodox tradition. Dr John and Mrs Grace Miles are very long-serving trustees. They are a retired couple who worked full-time for Brother Andrew's Open Doors. Also on our board is the Revd Tim Herbert, an experienced missionary who runs his own charity, with myself as chair of the charity. I am also responsible for its day-to-day running. Of the one hundred and thirty non-Slavic languages spoken by eighty-five million people of the former USSR population, IBT has now completed, after almost fifty years (as of 2023):

- Twelve full Bibles as modern, readable versions.
- Thirty New Testaments.
- Eighty Bible portions comprising one Gospel or less, some with only a few passages.
- Children's Bibles, also titled *The Bible in Pictures*, which has so far been published in more than fifty languages, with a total of over ten million copies. These are user-friendly and are well-read by adults.

IBT in Russia/CIS is currently working on almost fifty Bible translation projects and plans to complete a further twelve Bibles and/or New Testaments over the next ten years.

In 2016, we had a very special IBT year, where we completed and published, for the first time ever, the full Bible in the Uzbek, Tatar, Crimean Tatar, and Turkmen languages, which will potentially reach a further thirty-nine million people in their native language. It is a great and strategic work and I am deeply honoured to be a part of it. IBT's publishing work is currently presented in five formats: printing, download, apps, audio, and video clips with Scripture portions. The download and app versions are now reaching a high and increasing number. At this present time, the former Soviet Union has two regions which are partially or totally closed to Christianity; some areas of Central Asia (the 'stans) and the North Caucasus. The work of IBT however is as an academic, scientific organisation, not an overtly evangelistic one.

In the UK we have been honoured to be a part of IBT's international leadership since our foundation, as part of their International Association, which includes their supporting charities and others, including their International Advisory Board which advises the IBT Russia/CIS board. IBT adheres to the New Testament principle as demonstrated by St Paul, of healthy, missional, servant leadership, with the authority for the work being local where the responsibility is, rather than several thousand miles away. IBT did some re-structuring around this after the major part of the work was moved to Russia at the end of the Communist period. Once this restructuring had been completed, the work in Russia/CIS received a new impetus, as the foundation for another generation had been laid. We see the fruit of this now, with God's wonderful ongoing blessing upon the work.

Currently, part of my work involves succession planning in the UK, to pass on the UK charity to our younger trustees. We are in the middle of our five-year plan (a very Soviet concept!) and have already appointed some excellent younger trustees to continue the work. Our aim is that IBT UK will continue to be fully functional as a supporting charity for as long as IBT Russia/CIS exists. We expect the Bible translation work to continue at least until 2050. It is a long and laborious task and there are no quick solutions at this stage, such as an advanced Google Translate or an equivalent; the reason is that every language has its own complex rules. It takes on average twelve to fifteen years to translate the New Testament and twenty to twenty-five years to translate the complete Bible. The IBT leadership is very open to any future technological advances which might speed up the translation process. Perhaps at some stage, artificial intelligence (AI) could be used for a part of the process. We would be very open to such possibilities.

IBT works in the regions of the former Soviet Union, as follows:

1. The European part (Eastern Europe, Western Russia).
2. Siberia (where there are twenty-five native languages).

3. Central Asia (the 'stans).
4. The far north (including the Nenets, the 'Reindeer People').
5. The Far East (towards the Bering Strait).
6. The Caucasus (where there are forty-three native languages spoken in this closed mountainous region).

The traditional beliefs are mixed: many are Islamic (45 per cent of the languages), others are Animist or Shamanist (18 per cent), Atheist (14 per cent), Buddhist (2 per cent, three languages) and nominal Orthodox (21 per cent, many from two to three centuries ago).

The Caucasus region has been a massive challenge for IBT. It has been a major focus of our earnest and specific prayer since early 2014. Those within IBT (staff, co-workers, and supporters) have devoted the first or second day of every month to prayer and fasting for the peoples of this region, plus IBT's other regions. Since then (to 2023) we have received over two hundred major answers to prayer; such as a new exegetical checker in a particular language, or some other key prayer request, and at long last we are starting to see signs of a breakthrough, with new Bible translation projects being started. There is now also a prayer group somewhere in the world actively praying for each one of these forty-three people groups in the Caucasus region.

Those leading the Bible translation work have taken to heart: 'and with your blood you purchased for God persons from every tribe and language and people and nation,' (Revelation 5:9) and 'this gospel of the kingdom will be preached in the whole world as a testimony to all nations, and then the end will come,' (Matthew 24:14). We believe that God's strategic plan to reach all the unreached people groups is now well underway. This is a very exciting time for worldwide Christianity

A little bit about Moscow (pop. 12.7 million) itself; I have grown to really like the city, and it is fascinating to see people of so many nationalities walking or travelling around the city. Many of the multi-ethnic population in Moscow are actually indigenous. The Chinese-looking ones, for example, may not be Chinese; instead, they may be from the Altai Republic near Mongolia, or Dungan people from Kyrgyzstan. Peter I (the Great) and Catherine II expanded Russia to become a massive empire some three hundred years ago, between the seventeenth and nineteenth centuries, long before the Communist takeover and start of the USSR in 1917. This explains why we have all these indigenous, non-Slavic peoples living there. This fact is not widely known in the West, but it is the explanation for the one hundred and thirty indigenous people groups within this massive region.

I have to say that it hasn't all been hard work! Over the years I have greatly enjoyed the experience of the Bolshoi and other ballet performances with my Russian friends. They seem to know how to get cheap tickets. I have also enjoyed many trips on the Moscow River and seeing the main sights of Moscow. These include the Kremlin and St Basil's Cathedral in Red Square and other places of interest. Three of the more vivid memories of Moscow that stand out for me are, firstly, seeing a stunning performance of *Swan Lake* at the Bolshoi theatre; secondly, suddenly coming across a full philharmonic orchestra at the entrance to one of the magnificent Moscow Metro stations playing Beethoven's Ninth Symphony; and thirdly, visiting Lenin's tomb in Red Square. Outside this tomb was a Lenin-lookalike doing a wonderful acting job. He was so authentic; he was raking in the cash from the many visitors. I think he must be an oligarch by now!

One of my special memories is of the sheer beauty of St Andrew's Monastery, where IBT is based, nestled amongst the trees on the banks of the Moscow River. I have met so many lovely people there.

One particularly beautiful monastery service was held to celebrate thirty years of IBT, led by our wonderful Father Alexander who is the resident priest there and who is a gifted preacher. With the wonderful music, the choir, and the truly inter-denominational Christian congregation; it felt a bit like heaven. Just a bit more work to be done before then.

There is so much more that I could write, certainly about how God has guided IBT over many years. An account of God's help for IBT throughout, including its earlier days, has kindly been provided by Dr Borislav Arapović, IBT's founder. Having seen God powerfully at work in establishing and continuing IBT's Bible translation ministry, he has written:

> Any achievement, any step forward in IBT's almost half a century of existence to the present, is due to the Lord's hand in action. Ours are often only failures. The Lord's holy hand in the provision, guidance, protection, recruitment, finance, development, new locations, new translation projects, new doors, new ways, millions of printed copies, many conversions, etc.; a list of all this would be very, very long. The answer, the secret, to any success is in short; the Lord's holy hand.[3]

When IBT began its work in the early 1970s, the Soviet Union was one of the largest populations in the world without the New Testament or any other pages of the Bible translated into the numerous non-Slavic languages now targeted by IBT.[4] Bible translation during the post-Second World War period was well underway in many other parts of the world, but the Soviet

3. Borislav Arapović, personal communication.

4. Borislav Arapović, *Bibelns sidenväg*, 1998 (i.e. 'The Silk Road of the Bible'). Published in Swedish to mark IBT's twenty-fifth anniversary (1973–1998). Translated into English and due to be published.

Union, due to its Communist atheistic regime, was sealed off from such work.

Russia is the world's largest country by land mass (17,098,242 square kilometres). It is absolutely massive, stretching across eleven time zones between the Baltic and the Pacific oceans. It takes seven days and eight nights to travel the 5,772 miles (9,289 kilometres) from Moscow to Vladivostok on the Trans-Siberian Express train.[5] Most of the one hundred and thirty indigenous people groups, to whom IBT seeks to supply the Scriptures, live within the borders of the CIS.

The church in Russia has suffered some of the most severe and sustained persecution by any nation in recent history. It is estimated that between 1920 and 1990 there were twenty million deaths in the *gulags*, the prison camps, with a further sixteen million people who died in transit. Many were Christians. Two hundred thousand Christian leaders were martyred and a further 500,000 were imprisoned. In 1920, there were 100,000 church-owned buildings, but by 1940 these had been reduced to just a thousand, with the rest taken over or destroyed.[6]

The failed Communist atheistic ideology, which sought to completely destroy Christianity and resulted in seventy-six years of extreme persecution (promising to parade the USSR's last Christian on television), was finally destroyed by God answering the prayers of Christians who prayed for its overthrow. Of course, it was the millions of Christians in Russia who especially prayed, but they were joined by many others, including those involved in the seven years of prayer (organised by Open Doors) that began in 1982 and which we in St John's Church, Colchester, played a small part. After the overthrow of Communism, in

5. Caroline Eden, 'On Board the Trans-Siberian Railway for a Centenary Ride,' *The Guardian*, 12 November 2016.

6. Johnstone, Mandryk and Johnstone, *Operation World*.

the 1990s some 20 per cent of the Russian people moved from atheism to Christian belief within a short period of time.[7]

A few examples during IBT's early days will show God's holy hand at work. How, for instance, did IBT, at the time a small western Swedish organisation, find favour with the Russian Orthodox Church, with the Patriarch Alexiy II and with the Russian (at that time, USSR) Academy of Sciences early on in its existence? How was IBT able to move its work to St Andrew's Monastery in Moscow? IBT's close relations with Patriarch Alexiy II began on 4 November 1988 in Leningrad, while he was still the Metropolitan of Leningrad and Novgorod when Borislav and Peter van Driel (who was the chair of IBT's board, based in Sweden) were invited by the Russian Orthodox Church, as part of a fifteen-member delegation from the Nordic countries, to Russia to attend their thousand-year anniversary. A full programme included visits to various places in Moscow, to Zagorsk the nearby cloister town, then to Leningrad, where the delegation was received by the metropolitan (later the Patriarch Alexiy II) and other dignitaries. A major part of this visit and the reason for this invitation was to hand over the combined Nordic churches' Russian Orthodox millennial anniversary gift of 150,000 copies of *Tolkovaya Bibliya*, a three-volume study Bible with commentaries.

This gift was originally the idea and was then put together by IBT's Borislav and Peter van Driel. It was financed by the Nordic churches, Bible societies, east mission organisations, and several Nordic parliaments. Some eighteen months later, after the death of the previous Patriarch Pimen on 3 May 1990, Metropolitan Alexiy was elected to the patriarchal see of Moscow on 7 June 1990. Seven days after his election, Academician E. P. Chelyshev, a senior member of the USSR Academy of Sciences, who Borislav

7. Johnstone, Mandryk and Johnstone, *Operation World*.

had previously contacted in writing and who showed great interest in IBT's work, signed with Borislav in Moscow the Agreement on Collaboration between the Department of Literature and Language of the Academy of Sciences of the USSR and IBT. E. P. Chelyshev had very friendly relations with Patriarch Alexiy II and one can assume that IBT's friendship with the patriarch became even closer when the patriarch learned, maybe from E. P. Chelyshev, about IBT's relationship with the USSR Academy of Sciences. It is important to note that this was back in 1990 when the powerful Communist influence in USSR was still strong with its official teaching 'religion is the opium of the people' – and that IBT was a Western Christian organisation. IBT later had frequent audiences with the patriarch and also with E. P. Chelyshev.[8]

As the work expanded, first under the leadership of Vitali Zabavin, then from 1997 to 2013 under the leadership of Dr Marianne Beerle-Moor, and now under the leadership of Dr Vitaly Voinov, the need for more office space at a reasonable rate prompted Borislav, in August 1995, to write both to the patriarch and to the lord mayor of Moscow appealing for the provision of office facilities in Moscow for IBT, with E. P. Chelyshev and the Academy supporting these applications. About a year later, to IBT's great surprise, a message was received from the head of St Andrew's (Andreevsky) Monastery, Father Boris Danilenko, informing them that, in line with the wishes of the patriarch, IBT would be granted office quarters in the monastery, just a short walk from the newly built and massive Russian Academy of Sciences, which also houses IBT's joint-venture partners, the Department of Literature and Language.

St Andrew's Monastery was the perfect place for IBT to continue its work: their rent was only a fraction of office rents in Moscow,

8. Borislav Arapović, personal communication.
Borislav Arapović, *Bibelns sidenväg*.

IBT was given spacious offices, and it was here, in this very place, that in the seventeenth-century monks worked on the revision of the Church's Slavonic Bible texts, the Bible used in public church services, with history now repeating itself.[9] This was truly the hand of God and you could almost hear God saying: 'I have now placed you in this monastery in order to complete the Bible translation work which I did here in times past on behalf of the Russian peoples.' The result is that ever since 1996, with God's intervention (and assisted by the patriarch!), IBT has remained in the monastery and today still continues there with its far-reaching work.

Concluding Remarks From My Story

When I was converted at the age of twenty-three, I didn't realise that God would specifically 'call' me to anything in particular. I just served as best I could in small ways and in different areas. Indeed, having moved with Linda to Colchester and St John's Church in 1984, we both felt exactly the same. We certainly had not been involved in 'overseas mission'. When we started sending a few food parcels to our friend in Romania and Bibles to Russia and Romania, I genuinely thought that this would be it – the extent of our involvement in overseas mission. It is entirely due to the hand of God and to the prayers of my church family in St John's Church that I have been 'led' into even more productive pastures. I have to keep on pinching myself that God has called me into anything much at all. Well, if God can use me, then he can use anybody! I have had to learn to 'get into the car' and allow God to do the driving. I am unworthy; it is absurd that God uses me or any other human being to accomplish his will on Earth, but our sense of unworthiness before God is the qualification! I trust that the above account will show how God works through guidance and prayer,

9. Borislav Arapović, personal communication

combined with the teamwork of his people, in his church. Without a doubt, this journey has been far more about God than about me.

Why have I called this story *I Left My Hat in Moscow*? The fact is, I have always enjoyed wearing hats. Two years ago, I left my much-cherished Marks and Spencer trilby hat in St Andrew's Monastery in Moscow on my last night, so I had to return home without it. I didn't think much more about it, except having a strange feeling that something was 'about to happen.' Anyway, I gave my hat to a beloved and humble Orthodox brother in the monastery which was fine. Then, two days later, Linda went on her usual lunchtime walk at her place of work, to an isolated spot where nobody else ever visits. She saw this rather nice Ted Baker cap by the hedge. The thing is, she left it there for more than a day, thinking that somebody would claim it. But the place was so isolated and consequently, no one did. She felt sure that 'God had given it'. It was odd, but I received a wonderful replacement hat: a true gift from God, exactly the right size, and I have been wearing it ever since whenever I go outdoors.

Chapter Fifteen
How Can We Find God?

It is just wonderful that any one of us can, in this life, come to know God, which is to enter his kingdom, know without a shadow of a doubt that we are saved for eternity and will go to heaven when we die. For all who will accept Jesus into their lives, and without doing any good works whatsoever to earn this, it can become our experience. This is unadulterated good news! No wonder Jesus taught parables about the joy of finding enormous treasure, as in the parable of the man who finds treasure hidden in a field, and who then in his joy goes and sells all that he has in order to buy that field (Matthew 13:44). Similarly the parable of the merchant who finds a pearl of great price and sells all that he has to be able to buy it (Matthew 13:45–46). For the merchant in this story, this was surely the 'deal of a lifetime'.[1]

Our destiny for eternity rests entirely upon our individual response in this life to God's free offer of salvation. Blaise Pascal, the seventeenth-century French philosopher, in his famous wager, put forward the notion that every person, often without realising it, gambles with their lives that God either exists or does not.[2] The choice between these two destinies, heaven or hell (there is no purgatory, that is fiction), is entirely ours to make and is, therefore, a frightening

1. John Nolland, *The Gospel of Matthew: A Commentary on the Greek Text*. W. B. Eerdmans Publishing Co, 2005, pp.565–566.

2. James A. Connor, *Pascal's Wager: The Man Who Played Dice with God*. Lion Books, 2007, pp.180–181.

decision to make. That is why I show below how to accept Jesus as our Lord and Saviour, which is the right choice anyone can make.

A friend of mine recently wrote: 'You are not too dirty for God to cleanse, you are not too broken for God to fix, you are not too far for God to reach, you are not too guilty for God to forgive, and you are not too worthless for God to love.' I think that this statement is beautiful and it goes to the very heart of what God in Christ earnestly desires for each person on Earth; to receive God's offer of mercy and his offer to come and live within us. This is clear from the very nature of the incarnation; the divine condescension of Jesus the creator of the universe, to be born as a human being in order to die for our sins and to rise from the dead.

This was the divine lifeboat in action. Many passages from Scripture show the mercy of God: for example, the woman caught in adultery (John 7:53–8.11); the Samaritan woman at the well who had had five husbands (John 4:4–26); the parable of the tax collector who asked God to forgive him and received mercy, rather than the Pharisee who didn't (Luke 18:9–14). Perhaps one of the best-known parables is the story of the Prodigal Son (Luke 15:11–32). The story of the penitent thief on the cross alongside Christ's cross (Luke 23:40–43) shows that it is never too late in this life for anyone to receive God's mercy, that all are eligible and nobody is excluded. We are all, by nature, sinners in God's eyes, in thought, word, and deed, which condemns us all unless we receive God's mercy.

What happened to me when I was converted at the age of twenty-three? It was entirely unexpected, but I simply came to realise that I was a sinner who needed saving. I therefore accepted Jesus Christ as my Lord and Saviour. I repented and, by faith, personally surrendered to the lordship of Jesus Christ over my life. I then received this new divine life and found that, by God's mercy, the Holy Spirit, by invitation, had taken up residence within me so that I could truly say 'by the grace of God, I have the living Christ within'. That is momentous for any human being, and one immediate outcome was that I started receiving peace, joy, and reassurance from God.

What then are the key principles or steps to becoming a Christian? What are the A, B and C of this? Wonderfully, this can be done right now, it is as simple as that, and knowing this dispenses with all the complicated jargon that we humans often put in place which can cause more heat than light for anyone searching. Knowing these principles would have saved me from many years of searching. This is how it happens:

The first principle is that God loves every one of us; he created us, and we are made in God's image, with the capacity to personally know God. God loves us so fully and so completely that he also wishes to share his life with us. God has a plan for the rest of our life and for eternity, even if we know that we only have weeks or months left to live, and whatever our age, or however much we have messed up. God's entry into our life will, however, need to be by our individual invitation, it is not automatic, and as someone has said 'God is a gentleman', waiting to be invited.

The second principle is the 'sin' principle, in relation to God. That is, we can consider ourselves as reasonably good people in our own minds or in relation to others, and maybe we are, but what does God say? What is sin as defined by God and how could this possibly lead us to God's 'good news' or 'gospel' in a practical way? In the Scriptures, the law or divine standard is summarised in the Ten Commandments, with sin as the breaking of one or more of these. The standard of perfection required by God means that we are condemned by the breaking of just one of these Commandments, whether by thought, word, or deed. Deed alone condemns us all, but the addition of thought and word to this makes us even more aware of our abject failure before the holy God.

The apostle Paul writes in the book of Romans 3:10–12:

> As it is written: 'There is no one righteous, not even one; there is no one who understands; there is no one who seeks God. All have turned away, they have together become worthless; there is no one who does good, not even one.'

Again in Romans 3:20, Paul writes:

> Therefore no one will be declared righteous in God's sight by the works of the law; rather, through the law we become conscious of our sin. The prophet Isaiah says, 'But your iniquities have separated you from your God; your sins have hidden his face from you, so that he will not hear.'
>
> (Isaiah 59:2)

In other words, the Bible explains what the law is, but it also explains that all of us, without exception, have broken it. In no way can any one of us even attempt to keep God's law because we are all, by nature, destined to break it. It is a terrible predicament, and an awful indictment of our human condition. The apostle James writes 'for whoever keeps the whole law and yet stumbles at just one point is guilty of breaking all of it.' (James 2:10.)

Each one of us is, therefore, personally guilty and sinful before God, who is completely holy. Our utterly sinful, unholy, and hopeless condition should be understood before we can even begin to think about any solution.

The third principle is, thankfully, that of God's unique provision in Jesus Christ. It is wonderful that there is one, but only one, answer to our hopeless condition. God, in his love and mercy, provided the complete remedy for us by sending his only son, Jesus Christ, into the world to die for our sins and, by so doing, become our substitute by bearing the punishment for our sin. There are many verses from Scripture that explain what Jesus did on our behalf. Here are a few.

From the Old Testament:

> But he was pierced for our transgressions, he was crushed for our iniquities; the punishment that brought us peace was on him, and by his wounds we are healed. We all, like sheep, have gone astray, each of us has turned to our own way, and the Lord has laid on him the iniquity of us all.
>
> (Isaiah 53:5–6)

From the New Testament, just a few verses representing the many:

> She will give birth to a son, and you are to give him the name Jesus, because he will save his people from their sins.
>
> (Matthew 1:21)

> God made him who had no sin to be sin for us, so that in him we might become the righteousness of God.
>
> (2 Corinthians 5:21)

> This is my blood of the covenant, which is poured out for many for the forgiveness of sins.
>
> (Matthew 26:28)

> And he (Jesus) is the atoning sacrifice for our sins, and not only for ours but also for the sins of the whole world.
>
> (1 John 2:2)

In God's perfect love for us, his solution for our terrible, sinful condition was to send Jesus, his only son, into this world to shed his blood as the perfect sacrifice for sin and to be our substitute. Jesus was the only one able to do this because he was both God incarnate as well as fully human but was without sin. It underlines the catastrophic nature of our perilous condition that God had to go to such awful lengths. It demonstrates the immense love of God in that, rather than giving up on us, he initiated his plan of atonement in order to restore the broken relationship that began with Adam's sin as recorded in the book of Genesis and continues in each of our lives: our innate, original sin. In the Old Testament, innocent animals without blemish were offered to God as a blood sacrifice as atonement or 'covering' (the Hebrew word for atonement is *kaphar*, 'to cover'). During the Old Testament days, sin was provisionally covered through this sacrificial act of atonement, so that God no longer saw the sin (see Leviticus 1:4–5 and 17:11).

Later, at the right time and in a perfect way, Jesus the sinless and innocent one stood in our place and took the punishment that should have been ours. He shed his blood to pay for our sins and became the sacrifice of propitiation which satisfied God's wrath against sin. In Paul's letter to the Hebrews (9:12) it says, 'He [Jesus] did not enter by means of the blood of goats and calves; but he entered the Most Holy Place once for all by his own blood, thus obtaining eternal redemption.' Again, in 9:26b it says, 'But he has appeared once for all at the culmination of the ages to do away with sin by the sacrifice of himself.'

The fourth principle is that each of us needs to make our personal response. We have seen something of our own sinfulness compared with the unapproachable holiness of God, that the two are inherently incompatible. *But* in the loving-kindness and mercy of God, he sent Jesus to be the perfect sacrificial substitute for our sins. This means that we can now choose life rather than death and heaven rather than hell, but only on one condition; that we accept Jesus Christ,

God's Holy One, as our Lord and Saviour. The first step is personal repentance for our own sinfulness and then our acceptance of the finished work of Jesus Christ on our behalf. Once we have sincerely done this, we will receive the Holy Spirit who will live in us for the rest of our lives and do his divine work within us.

We can then start to be changed from within, and begin to live a life that is pleasing to God. The Scriptures are very clear that to become right or be reconciled with God, we need to first accept the finished work of Jesus on the cross. This salvation is a free gift that begins with a simple prayer of repentance and faith. Thus begins a wonderful new personal relationship with God. It really is very simple. I might add that this is very practical and it works. It happened to me at the age of twenty-three and, throughout the past forty-seven years since, I have experienced the joy of having the living Christ within. He is the one who has stayed closer than a brother to help, comfort, and guide me, as I have explained in my own story in this book. The experience described by St Paul in 2 Corinthians 4:7 has become mine: 'But we have this treasure in jars of clay to show that this all-surpassing power is from God and not from us.' This is true of all those who believe and have received God's salvation, to the glory of God.

A Prayer of Repentance

With God's loving provision of Jesus Christ as our sin substitute, we can now pray a prayer of repentance and faith. I offer this example:

> Lord Jesus Christ, I am sorry for the things that I have done wrong in my life. I ask for your forgiveness and now turn away from everything which I know is wrong. Thank you for dying on the

> cross for me to set me free from my sins. Please come into my life and fill me with your Holy Spirit and be with me forever. Thank you, Lord Jesus. Amen.[3]

Such is the love of God for us that simply praying and *meaning* this prayer, without any good works on our part whatsoever, is all that we need to be transferred, immediately and forever, from the kingdom of darkness into the kingdom of light. We are now real Christians, saved solely by the finished work of Christ on the cross. Nothing else is required of us for our salvation, except to continue believing and trusting that God has done all the work for us. This was always God's redemptive plan; it is as simple and beautiful as this. We are now covered by the righteousness and sacrifice of Christ himself so that from now on, with the sin barrier removed, God will always see in us the righteousness of Christ. We are then 'in Christ'; such is the mercy of God towards us.

If you have taken this step of faith and prayed the prayer, I congratulate you. You have not only been forgiven but you have now been declared righteous and have become a child of God. It is a wonderful, amazing entry into a new life, a new realm, in which you will receive all of God's blessings, now that the sin barrier has been removed. As an integral part of our Christian conversion, we also receive what is known as 'justification by faith alone.' I wish to explain this below.

My wife, Linda, and I were immensely privileged to attend the five hundredth anniversary of the Reformation in Westminster Abbey in October 2017. This was to celebrate the rediscovery by Martin Luther of that wonderful key Christian doctrine called 'justification by faith alone' which has always been crystal clear

3. *Begin Your Journey to Peace.* Peace with God, Billy Graham Evangelistic Association UK, 2021.

from the Scriptures but somehow was lost in the Middle Ages. This teaching, which runs right through the Scriptures, is simple: it is that our salvation depends entirely upon Christ's mercy, which solely comes through personal faith and without any good deeds by us. It is also fully backed up by the confessions of major church denominations. For example in the 'Thirty-nine Articles of Religion' of the Church of England and the 'Westminster Confession of Faith' of the Presbyterian Church.

This is what Martin Luther wrote in the Augsburg Confession, Article IV, in 1530:

> It is also taught among us that we cannot obtain forgiveness of sin and righteousness before God by our own merits, works, or satisfactions, but that we receive forgiveness of sin and become righteous before God by grace, for Christ's sake, through faith, when we believe that Christ suffered for us and that for his sake our sin is forgiven and righteousness and eternal life are given to us. For God will regard and reckon this faith as righteousness, as Paul says in Romans 3:21–26 and 4:5.

To quote a few of the verses in Scripture illustrating this teaching, leaving no doubt that this is the only way to receive salvation from God:

> However, to the one who does not work but trusts God who justifies the ungodly; their faith is credited as righteousness.
>
> (Romans 4:5)

> And be found in him, not having a righteousness of my own that comes from the law, but that which is through faith in Christ – the righteousness that comes from God on the basis of faith.
>
> (Philippians 3:9)

> For it is by grace you have been saved, through faith – and this is not from yourselves, it is the gift of God – not by works, so that no one can boast.
>
> (Ephesians 2:8–9)

> Yet we know that a person is not justified by works of the law, but by faith in Jesus Christ. So we, too, have put our faith in Christ Jesus that we may be justified by faith in Christ and not by works of the law, because by the works of the law no one will be justified.
>
> (Galatians 2:16)

> God made him who had no sin to be sin for us, so that in him we might become the righteousness of God.
>
> (2 Corinthians 5:21)

> He saved us, not because of righteous things we had done, but because of his mercy. He saved us through the washing of rebirth and renewal by the Holy Spirit.
>
> (Titus 3:5)

It is clear from these verses that we are all sinners and completely helpless to save ourselves. But we can be saved; this is of course God's earnest desire and the reason for Christ's incarnation, but only through the perfect and finished work of Jesus Christ. This is received solely by faith, and not by any works on our part. This is how to become reconciled to God and receive true peace in our hearts and minds, and everlasting salvation.

In the following section, I will move way beyond my own story or testimony and provide further evidence for God's existence by looking at Christian Revival. These sovereign, supernatural, and life-changing interventions by God, often upon whole nations, have occurred throughout Christian history in many countries. In Wales, my own nation, there were no less than fifteen of these over a period of a hundred and fifty years.

PART TWO

THE EVIDENCE FROM CHRISTIAN REVIVALS

When the day of Pentecost came, they were all together in one place. Suddenly a sound like the blowing of a violent wind came from heaven and filled the whole house where they were sitting. They saw what seemed to be tongues of fire that separated and came to rest on each of them. All of them were filled with the Holy Spirit and began to speak in other tongues as the Spirit enabled them.

(Acts 2:1–4)

Those who accepted his message were baptised, and about three thousand were added to their number that day.

(Acts 2:41)

Chapter Sixteen
Revivals Impact upon Wales

In this section, I will provide further evidence for God's existence through his work in Christian revivals. A revival is a supernatural, sovereign act of God. It is a life-changing event for all involved, as is evident from Letterston, a large village close to where I was brought up, between 1905 and 1910. It had a long-lasting effect on this large village. It happens when God's power comes down and many people over a period of weeks, months, and occasionally years are drawn in and converted to Christ. Revivals occur when God's people, the Church, take the Bible and God's promises seriously and pray fervently, often for many years, for such outpourings to occur.

One cannot help but be profoundly moved when reading accounts of the way God's awesome power has come down at different times throughout Christian history. As a person of Welsh heritage, these sovereign, supernatural interventions of God are particularly precious; not least because the last Welsh revival impacted my local village and its surrounding area. I write about deeply holy matters and words are really inadequate when trying to explain God's outpourings during these special times.

We can read all that we need to know about God, his character and how he works in the pages of the Bible. Christian revivals are further powerful evidence of his work in special ways throughout the world. The first and greatest revival ever seen was the birth of the Christian church itself, which is recorded in the New Testament book of Acts 2:1–47. This occurred in Jerusalem on the Jewish feast day of Pentecost. About a hundred and twenty disciples of Jesus Christ gathered in an upper room, dramatically received the Holy Spirit and within just a few hours three thousand people were added to their number. This outpouring of God resulted in the church's rapid growth which spread to the key cities of the Roman Empire and then throughout the known world. Thus the Christian church was established. Truly, the revival of all revivals!

What is perhaps less well known is that revivals have also occurred in different places, regions, and countries at many different times since then. I personally know people who have been involved in revivals in China (the 1980s), East Africa (1940s), the Hebrides (1950), Romania (1970s) and Finland (2000s). But, that is just the tip of a massive iceberg and within my own very limited experience.

In Wales, where I am from, there were no less than fifteen revivals between the mid-1700s and 1862, earning Wales the reputation as 'the land of revivals'.[1] There were three very large ones: in 1739, 1859 and 1904. The 1904 revival came to my local village of Letterston, just three miles from my home. This outpouring of God was so powerful that some five years later, in 1910, every family, except one, out of Letterston's almost one thousand population, either went to church or to chapel, that is St Giles (Anglican), Saron (Welsh Baptist) or Horeb (Congregationalist).[2] It was similar elsewhere and the spiritual effects were relatively long-lasting and were not simply a flash of emotionalism in the heat of the moment which quickly blew over.

The last major Welsh revival initially began to break out in New

1. Larry V. Brown, *A History of Christianity in Wales*. 11 May 2008, p.6.

2. Revd. W. G. R. (Bill) Lewis, personal communication. The Revd Bill Lewis was formerly the vicar of St Giles Church, Letterston. This was a conversation he had in the 1970s with Mr Jones the coalman, from Letterston, of his recollection as a young man in 1910. I too knew Mr Jones, who delivered coal to our farm in the 1950s and 1960s.

Quay, Cardiganshire, in February 1904 and spread to other parts of Wales during that year. I am most grateful to David Edward Pike for providing the following information in his excellent and detailed blog, 'By the middle of January 1905, the revival in our part of Wales had been going on for at least six weeks.' It is recorded that on one Sunday in January 1905, thirty-two new members of Saron Baptist Chapel, Letterston, were baptised before a large gathering by the Revd B. Thomas the pastor, assisted by the Revd Dan Davies. Several of the candidates were of advanced age – over seventy – and notwithstanding the keen biting wind, submitted to what must have been a trying experience with 'fervent eagerness'. Comparable events were taking place almost simultaneously in other places. For example, the following day ninety-four converts were baptised in the River Gwaun in Lower Fishguard. They were from Hermon Baptist Church, Fishguard.

Hermon Baptist, under the leadership of the Revd Dan Davies, saw membership of that chapel reach seven hundred and forty-eight, in spite of twice sending out significant numbers to support church planting elsewhere. Another recorded example was at Harmony Baptist Chapel, Pencaer, near Fishguard, where forty converts were baptised at around the same time. To put this into context, that number would have been almost the entire population of this rural community! We have these accounts from my own rather isolated locality from around January in 1905; astonishingly, thirty-two from one village, ninety-four from another, and forty from a third, in just a few weeks. In our locality, God had come down and was moving powerfully, as in other parts of Wales.[3]

3. David Edward Pike, 'Outbreak of Revival in North Pembrokeshire in 1904'. Last modified 10 February 2012. https://www.daibach-welldigger.blogspot.com/2012/02/revival-in-north-pembrokeshire-in-1904.html.

I am grateful for the helpful article by Tony Cauchi 'The Welsh Revival – 1904' for the following information, unless otherwise cited.[4]

The 1904–5 Welsh revival was a spiritual awakening that began under the leadership of Evan Roberts, a twenty-six-year-old former collier from Loughor, near Swansea. The outpouring lasted for up to two years, during which time 100,000 people from Wales were converted, out of a total population of around two million. Evan Roberts was certainly the pioneer of this great revival. Although still only a young man, he had already been praying for revival and an outpouring of the Holy Spirit for thirteen years, from his early teens. On 22 September 1904, he received a special anointing from God on a day of prayer and fasting, which was the start of the major part of the revival. A little later he received a vision from God that through this outpouring God would win 100,000 souls, which came to pass. He returned home to Loughor from Newcastle Emlyn where he had been enrolled in Bible College.

During his first few meetings, the heavens opened and God's presence seemed to fill the air. A major feature of the services was a terrible conviction of sin. Others cried for mercy and many were so filled with God's Holy Spirit that they pleaded with God to 'stay his hand.'[5] Shortly after this, the revival spread to other places in South Wales and, later, to North Wales. The 100,000 people were converted within six months; such was the effect of the outpouring.

Evan Roberts was a young man of great sincerity who relied upon the immediate guidance of the Holy Spirit. He was very conscious that he was an instrument being used by God and he

4. Tony Cauchi, 'The Welsh Revival – 1904', The Revival Library. https://www.revival-library.org/revival_histories/evangelical/1900/welsh_revival_1904.shtml

5. Cauchi, 'The Welsh Revival – 1904'.

often said, 'This movement is not of me, it is of God. I would not dare direct it – it is the Spirit alone who is leading us.'[6] It is significant that God did not choose a church dignitary or a Bible scholar to lead this movement, but a young man who leaned upon God and who got out of the way in order to allow God to lead and to do the work. His attitude was that all the glory and the credit should go to God. The revival was characterised by hymn singing, prayer, personal conviction, testimony, and miraculous events, which was somewhat different from the powerful preaching of earlier revivals. It is also significant that the revival came upon all the Christian denominations, both church (Anglican) and chapel (Nonconformist). It had a unifying effect on the whole church.

Dr Campbell Morgan of Westminster Chapel, London, visited the revival meetings and was stirred by its intensity. He reported,

> It is Pentecost continued, without a single moment's doubt. The meetings are absolutely without order, characterised from the first to the last by the orderliness of the Spirit of God. There were organs, but they were silent; ministers, but they were not preaching. Among the rest of the people, there was rejoicing and prophesying. Yet the Welsh Revival is the revival of preaching in Wales. Everyone it seems is preaching. No order, and yet it moves from day to day with matchless precision, with the order of an attacking force.[7]

Here are a few stories about the effects of the revival:

A young man called Tom Hughes from Aberdare, previously a convinced atheist but now a converted Christian, burned his books

6. Patrick Slattery, 'The Legacy of the Welsh Revival 1904–1905', *Headline*, summer 2004, Methodist Evangelicals Together (MET), pp.16–17.

7. Slattery, 'The Legacy of the Welsh Revival,' p.17.

of unbelief and is now working day and night for those who, like him, belonged to the so-called Ethical Society.[8]

Down in the mines, the horses were terribly puzzled. A manager said, 'The hauliers are some of the very lowest. They have driven their horses by obscenity and kicks. Now they can hardly persuade the horses to start working because there is no obscenity and no kicks.'[9]

The Cardiff police reported a 60 per cent decrease in drunkenness and 40 per cent fewer people in jail in the new year of 1905; the great wave of sobriety that swept over Wales caused severe financial losses to the liquor trade and closed many of the taverns which became bankrupt.

Judges had no cases to be tried; by December 1904 the police were out of work. Instead, they went with the crowds and formed quartets to sing during church services.

The illegitimate birth rate dropped 44 per cent in two counties within a year of the start of the revival.

Political meetings and even football matches were postponed.

Employers noticed a great improvement in the work produced by their employees.[10]

There was a story told in a Wrexham newspaper of a Christian man from Barrow-in-Furness, Lancashire, who had read about the revival in his daily newspaper in the summer of 1905 and decided to see for himself what was happening.[11] He arrived at Chester station with his two daughters and asked the porter: 'How do we get to the place where the revival is?' The porter told them that there would

8. William T. Stead, G. Campbell Morgan, Arthur Goodrich, Evan Roberts, *The Welsh Revival & the Story of the Welsh Revival: As Told by Eyewitnesses Together With a Sketch of Evan Roberts and His Message to the World.* Trumpet Press, August 2015.

9. Stead, Campbell Morgan, Goodrich, Roberts, *The Welsh Revival.*

10. Chet and Phyllis Swearingen, *The Welsh Revival of 1904–05.* Beautiful Feet Inc, IN 46706, USA. March 2018. https://www. romans1015.com/welsh-revival-1904–05/.

11. Dave Edwards, 'A Spiritual Awakening was Taking Place in Rhos – Welsh Revival 1904–5,' *Wrexham History.* https://www.wrexham-history.com/the-1904–5-welsh-revival/

be a train at 8.00 am to Wrexham and from there they could catch a local train to Rhos, which was one of the revival's local epicentres. 'But how will we know when we are near Wrexham?' they asked. 'Oh,' replied the porter, 'you'll feel it in the train.' And they did! They sensed an unmistakable expectancy in the air. Two miles outside Rhos they enquired again and were told, 'Go down that road and you will feel it down there.' It was 9:00 am on a Monday when the visitor and his two daughters arrived at the chapel to find it already full of worshippers who had been there since 7:00 am.

The 1904 revival had a huge impact on the church in other places. It is regarded as the most widespread of all revivals and stimulated much prayer in the Christian world. This increased prayer ignited revivals in other areas. In the UK it is estimated that over a million people became Christians as a result. Shortly after this revival, there were others in Scandinavia, Germany, Austria, Poland, Slovakia, Hungary, the Balkans and Russia.

Chapter Seventeen
Previous Revivals and Their Effects

To emphasise the way that God has continued to revive his church over the centuries since the time of Pentecost, here is a potted summary of some major post-Reformation ones, some key participants, and their effects. Again, I am grateful to Tony Cauchi for this information unless otherwise cited:[1]

The First Great Awakening, from 1727–1766: this is the well-known Wesley-Whitefield revival. The start of this goes back to the Moravian community. Count von Zinzendorf of Herrnhut, Saxony, was the leader of this movement that began a twenty-four-hour-a-day prayer meeting, which extraordinarily continued non-stop for over a hundred years! By 1791, sixty-five years after the start of that prayer vigil, this small Moravian community (initially only three hundred people) had sent out three hundred missionaries to the ends of the Earth.[2] As in all things Christian, prayer is required and God will answer. Perhaps it could also be suggested that the greater the prayer, normally the more pronounced the results.

This first great awakening also involved the well-known Jonathan Edwards, in addition to George Whitefield and John Wesley, who had become good friends while studying at Oxford in the 1730s.

1. Tony Cauchi, 'The Six Major Revival Waves', The Revival Library. https://www.revival-library.org/index.shtml

2. Leslie K. Tarr, 'A Prayer Meeting that Lasted 100 Years,' *Christian History*. https://www.christianhistoryinstitute.org/magazine/article/one-hundred-year-prayer-meeting.

Whitefield preached in almost every town in England, Scotland and Wales, and crossed the Atlantic seven times. He preached an estimated 18,000 sermons, with great results. Wesley was an itinerant preacher for sixty-five years. It is recorded that he travelled around 250,000 miles on horseback and preached some 40,000 sermons! He wrote 233 books plus a complete commentary on the whole Bible. He left behind him 750 preachers in England, 350 in America and, with Charles Wesley his brother, 9,000 hymns were written. Although he remained an Anglican throughout his life, his legacy was the formation of the Methodist Church.

The Second Great Awakening was from 1792 to the 1820s. This revival resulted in the founding of the British and Foreign Bible Society, the Religious Tract Society, the Baptist Missionary Society and the Church Missionary Society, amongst many others. It also produced great social reforms such as the abolition of the slave trade, prison reform, the start of the Sunday School movement and others.

The Third Great Awakening was from 1830 to the early 1840s. This was also international. In the UK it saw the founding of the Brethren Movement, with such notable people as J. N. Darby and George Müller. The latter pioneered orphanage work in Bristol and set out to prove to the Christian world that God answers specific prayers. From his diaries, it is estimated that God answered over 50,000 specific prayers during his lifetime.[3] He in turn has had a major impact on many since then, right up to this day. In Wales during this period the preachers John Elias, Christmas Evans, and William Williams also had a great impact.

The Fourth Great Awakening, from 1857 onwards, was again international in scope and massive in scale. It began in Canada and then moved to America. Within two years, this initially lay-led movement resulted in a million converts in the Americas.

3. Roger Steer, *George Müller: Delighted in God.* Christian Focus, 20 March 2015.

In the UK there were also great effects from 1859 onwards. This was the largest Welsh revival prior to 1904, where from February 1859 around 110,000 people were converted in the space of twelve months. In England, half a million people were converted, 30,000 in Scotland, and 100,000 in Ulster. This revival led to the founding of the Salvation Army by William and Catherine Booth and the arrival of great preachers; notably Charles Haddon Spurgeon in the UK. The China Inland Mission was founded by Hudson Taylor. Further fruit was the social work of Lord Shaftsbury, Dr Barnardo's orphanages, and the missionary work of David Livingstone in Africa.[4]

The Fifth Great Awakening was from 1880 onwards. This included the work of D. L. Moody, who travelled the world with his singing evangelistic companion Ira Sankey. Moody and Sankey's evangelistic work in the UK was very successful. It saw the establishment of the YMCA and the Christian Union. Also, what is known as the Cambridge Seven, including C. T. Studd, undertook mission work in China from 1885. C. T. Studd also later founded WEC, the Worldwide Evangelistic Crusade.

The Sixth Great Awakening resulted in the 1904–5 Welsh revival and in 1906 in Los Angeles, USA, the emergence of the modern Pentecostal movement which continues as the fastest growing church in Africa.

Finally, a moving story about a very special young man who was the product of one of these early Welsh revivals and who is almost forgotten in his home country but is rightly considered a hero amongst Korean Christians. His name is Robert Jermain Thomas, and this story was first related to me by my South Korean missionary friend, Dr Guichun Jun. I am grateful to Faith Cook and to Eliezer

4. Tony Cauchi, 'The Fourth Great Awakening – 1857 Onwards', The Revival Library. https://www.revival-library.org/revival_histories/evangelical/1857/1857.shtml

Gonzalez for their written accounts of what happened and whose material I use below.[5] Robert Thomas was born in 1839, the son of a Welsh Congregational minister, and was brought up in Llanover, near Abergavenny. He was educated at Llandovery College and was gifted in languages, graduating from New College, London, and winning the prize as the most outstanding student of his year.

He was ordained in June 1863 and, turning his back upon a promising career, joined the London Missionary Society in order to bring the gospel to China. He and his young wife, Caroline, arrived in Shanghai after a five-month sea voyage. Shortly after, his pregnant wife and developing child suddenly and tragically died. Nevertheless, Robert Thomas pressed on with his missionary calling. While in China, Robert heard of Korea, which was then known as the 'Hermit Kingdom' having no contact with outsiders.[6] He made a secret visit in 1865 taking with him Chinese Bibles. Those who received the Bibles risked death if they were discovered. In 1866 Robert returned to Korea aboard an American trading ship, taking more Bibles with him.

Near Pyongyang, now the capital of North Korea, the ship ran aground and was set on fire by Korean fire rafts. Standing on the burning deck Robert flung the Bibles into the water hoping that they would float ashore and be read by the people. He then, with his clothes on fire, jumped overboard offering his remaining Bibles. A boy of twelve grabbed three of the Bibles and ran off. Others also picked up the books that Robert dropped. The boy who had taken the three Bibles gave them to a soldier who tore out the pages and

5. Faith Cook, 'Of Whom the World Was Not Worthy – Robert Thomas,' *Evangelical Times*, September 1997. https://www.evangelical-times.org/articles/historical/of-whom-the-world-was-not-worthy-2/

Eliezer Gonzalez, 'The Story of Robert Thomas – Martyr in Korea,' Good News Unlimited, 31 March 2020. https://www.goodnewsunlimited.com/the-story-of-robert-thomas-martyr-in-korea/

6. https://en.wikipedia.org/wiki/Robert_Jermain_Thomas

used them to wallpaper his home. The boy himself later became a Christian, as did others. Although the Korean officialdom tried to gather up and burn all the literature that Robert had brought, some escaped their notice and were read in secret. Even the wallpaper proved powerful to the conversion of another. There are several differing accounts of how Robert Thomas was martyred at only twenty-seven years of age.

When some twenty years later missionaries finally gained access to the country, they found small groups of Christians in the towns along the riverside where Robert had thrown his Bibles. In Pyongyang, a church had already been founded. Robert Thomas's life and work were not in vain. This is a wonderful example of that great saying by Tertullian (c.155–c.225 AD), one of the early church fathers, that 'the blood of the martyrs is the seed of the church'. Today, the Christian church in South Korea numbers many millions and includes some of the largest evangelical churches in the world. This all started with one young man, Robert Jermain Thomas, who sacrificed his life for the sake of the Korean people.

PART THREE

APOLOGETIC EVIDENCE
Old Testament Prophecies Fulfilled

Chapter Eighteen
Jesus the Messianic Fulfilment

> For prophecy never had its origin in the human will, but prophets, though human, spoke from God as they were carried along by the Holy Spirit.
>
> (2 Peter 1:21)

As my third key evidence for God's existence, as well as for the supernatural, divine nature of the Bible itself, I will look at the fulfilment of what is known as the Messianic prophecies written in the Old Testament and literally fulfilled hundreds of years later by Jesus himself. Amongst the top questions that many of us ask when thinking about God would be: how do we know that God exists? How can Christians say that their religion is the only true one? How can the Bible be trusted? Don't all religions lead to the same God?[1] These are valid questions and the answers can be found by looking at the many Messianic prophecies written about the person, life, and ministry of Jesus Christ in the Old Testament more than four hundred and fifty years before they occurred.

There are over three hundred and fifty such prophecies, many very specific and verified in the New Testament. The detailed fulfilment of these prophecies is quite extraordinary and therefore begs further valid questions. Could they have been the result of self-fulfilment or manipulation? Could they have been so general, analogous to fortune-

1. 'Top Ten Questions College Students Ask About God and the Christian Faith,' Cruatunc.com/hp_Wordpress, August 2013, pp.1–5.

telling, that they didn't prove anything? Could these prophecies have been added to after the events? I will try to address these points in this section. I believe that any real faith in God can be supported by solid evidence and reason, properly explored. Christianity has never been about mythology or fairy tales. We are not expected to have 'blind faith.' Thankfully, the ground on which we are treading is solid, it is open to scrutiny and it should be examined. The experience over many centuries is that the deeper we probe, the more solid we find this ground and evidence to be.

What Does the Bible Say About Prophecy?

The Bible laid out its own test when God himself made his challenge to the false Babylonian idol-gods and their inability to predict future events. These dumb idols that the heathen worshipped knew nothing about future events, they could not predict them and still less could they control them.[2] God addressed them through Isaiah, one of his prophets:

> Present your case,' says the Lord. 'Set forth your arguments,' says Jacob's King. 'Tell us, you idols, what is going to happen. Tell us what the former things were, so that we may consider them and know their final outcome. Or declare to us the things to come, tell us what the future holds, so we may know that you are gods. Do something, whether good or bad, so that we will be dismayed and filled with fear.
>
> (Isaiah 41:21–23)

None of these other 'gods', religions, or belief systems, whether at that time, since then, or now, in the twenty-first century, have been

2. Arno C. Gaebelein, 'Fulfilled Prophecy a Potent Argument for the Bible,' in *The Fundamentals*, ed. R. A. Torrey. https://www.blueletterbible.org/Comm/torrey_ra/fundamentals/25.cfm

able to either foretell the future or provide a genuine relationship with the real God. The sole revelation of the one true God is found exclusively in the Bible. It stands alone as the only book in existence that is primarily prophetic in character and which contains the words of God himself. It is a supernatural book, clearly explaining God's revelation to humanity. It has been proven to be true, not least because of its many fulfilled prophecies about Jesus Christ and his coming, predicted more than four hundred and fifty years before they occurred.

This is what Jesus himself said about these same Scriptures when he revealed himself to two of his disciples travelling home on the road from Jerusalem to Emmaus, immediately after his resurrection:

> How foolish you are, and how slow to believe all that the prophets have spoken! Did not the Messiah have to suffer these things and then enter his glory? And beginning with Moses and all the Prophets, he explained to them what was said in all the Scriptures concerning himself.
>
> (Luke 24:25–27)

Here is a further example from the words of Jesus, confirming that he was the fulfilment of these ancient prophecies:

> Do not think that I have come to abolish the Law or the Prophets; I have not come to abolish them but to fulfil them.
>
> (Matthew 5:17)

As a Jew, Jesus was well-versed in the Hebrew Bible (now our Old Testament), even at the age of twelve sitting in the temple courts of Jerusalem, listening to the teachers and asking them questions, with everyone being amazed at his understanding and his answers (Luke 2:39–50).

What Are These Prophecies?

Here are some of these key prophecies, so accurate that it was either God knowing and determining the future, or these sacred writings were somehow tampered with. There is, in my opinion, no third option. We can group these Messianic prophecies into four main categories. For the sake of brevity I have listed one Old Testament prophecy and one New Testament fulfilment, as some fulfilments are included several times in the New Testament:

1. Those relating to Jesus's birth.
2. Jesus's ministry on Earth.
3. Jesus's death and resurrection.
4. Jesus's role in the church.

1. Jesus's Birth

Jesus was predicted to come from the line of Abraham: Genesis 22:18; Matthew 1:1.

Jesus would be descended from Isaac, not from Ishmael, another son of Abraham: Genesis 17:19; Luke 3:34.

Jesus would be descended from Jacob, not from Isaac's other brother, Esau: Numbers 24:17; Matthew 1:2; then in turn from Judah, not from one of Jacob's other eleven sons: Genesis 49:10; Luke 3:3.

Jesus would be descended from the royal house of David and be heir to his throne, only it would be an eternal one: Isaiah 9:7; Luke 1:32–33.

Jesus would be born of a woman: Genesis 3:15; Matthew 1:20.

Jesus would be born of a virgin: Isaiah 7:14: Luke 2:4–6.

Jesus would be born in Bethlehem: Micah 5:2; Luke 2:4–6.

Jesus would spend time in Egypt: Hosea 11:1; Matthew 2:14–15.

A massacre of children would take place in Bethlehem, the place of his birth: Jeremiah 31:15; Matthew 2:16–18.

2. Jesus's Ministry on Earth

Jesus was predicted to be preceded by a messenger: Isaiah 40:3–4; John 1.23.

Jesus' ministry would begin in Galilee: Isaiah 9:1–2; Matthew 4:12–17.

Jesus would be made humble and become human to fulfil his work: Psalm 8:5–6; Hebrews 2:5–9.

Jesus would destroy the devil's work: Genesis 3:15; 1 John 3:8.

Jesus would live a sinless, unblemished life: Exodus 12:5; Hebrews 9:14.

Jesus would be a prophet: Deuteronomy 18:15; Acts 3:20–22.

Jesus would perform miracles: Isaiah 35:5–6; Matthew 11:2–6.

Jesus would be sent to heal the broken hearted: Isaiah 61:1–2; Luke 4:18–19.

Jesus would come in gentleness: Isaiah 42:1–4; Matthew 12:15–21.

Jesus would be praised by little children: Psalm 8:2; Matthew 21:16.

Jesus would teach in parables: Psalm 78:1–2; Matthew 13:34–35.

Jesus's parables would fall on deaf ears: Isaiah 6:9–10; Matthew 13:13–15.

Jesus would be despised and rejected by his own people: Isaiah 53:3; Luke 4:28–29.

Jesus would draw the Gentiles (non-Jews) to himself: Isaiah 11:10; John 12:18–21.

Jesus would free the captives: Isaiah 61:1; Luke 4:16–21.

Jesus would put an end to sin: Daniel 9:24; Galatians 1:3–5.

Jesus would have an everlasting kingdom: Daniel 7:13–14; Luke 1:31–33.

Jesus would enter Jerusalem riding on a donkey: Zechariah 9:9; Matthew 21:8–10.

Jesus would be betrayed for thirty pieces of silver: Zechariah 11:12–13; Matthew 27:6–10.

3. Jesus's Death and Resurrection

Jesus was predicted to be quiet before his accusers: Psalm 38:12–13; Matthew 27:12–14.
Jesus would be mocked and abused: Isaiah 50:3–6; Matthew 27:27–31.
Jesus would be forsaken or abandoned: Psalm 22:1; Matthew 27:46.
Jesus would be held in contempt: Psalm 22:8; Matthew 27:42–43.
Jesus would be crucified with criminals: Isaiah 53:12; Matthew 27:38.
Jesus's suffering would involve thirst: Psalm 22:15; John 19:28.
Jesus's thirst would be quenched with vinegar and gall: Psalm 69:21; Matthew 27:34.
Jesus would be forsaken by God: Psalm 22:1; Matthew 27:46.
Jesus would pray for his enemies: Psalm 109:4; Luke 23:24.
Jesus would cry out, 'Into your hands I commit my spirit': Psalm 31:5; Luke 23:46.
Jesus's hands and feet would be pierced: Psalm 22:16; John 19:36–37.
Jesus would be the Passover Lamb: Exodus 12:21–27; 1 Corinthians 5:7.
None of Jesus's bones would be broken, as with the Passover Lamb: Exodus 12:46; John 19:31–36.
Jesus's blood would be given for atonement: Leviticus 17:11; Matthew 26:28.
Jesus would become a perfect sacrifice: Psalm 40:6–8; Hebrews 10:5–10.
Soldiers would gamble for Jesus's garments: Psalm 22:18; John 19:23–24.
Jesus would be buried with the rich: Isaiah 53:9; Matthew 27:57–60.
Jesus would rise from the dead: Psalm 16:10; Mark 16: 1–14.
Jesus's resurrection was predicted: Psalm 118:17–18; Luke 25:5–7.
Jesus would conquer death: Isaiah 25:7–8; 1 Corinthians 15:54.
Jesus would ascend into heaven: Psalm 68:18; Ephesians 4:7–16.

4. Jesus's Role in the Church

Jesus was predicted to be God's everlasting High Priest: 1 Samuel 2:35; Hebrews 2:17.
Jesus would be seated at God's right hand: Psalm 68:18; Mark 16:19.
Jesus would judge the world with justice: Psalm 9:7–10; Acts 17:31.
Jesus would have full authority, including in judgement: Isaiah 22:22; Revelation 3:7.
Jesus would pour out the Holy Spirit: Isaiah 44:3; John 16:7.
Jesus would make a new covenant with his people: Jeremiah 31:31; Matthew 26:28.

NOTE: for a more detailed reflection I recommend two articles: firstly from the Jesus Film organisation, *55 Old Testament Prophecies About Jesus,* Jesus Film Project, 4 January 2018. Secondly, for a more complete list of the three hundred and fifty-one fulfilled Old Testament prophecies: David Webb, *351 Old Testament Prophecies Fulfilled in Jesus Christ,* 17 May 2021.

What Should We Make of the Above?

I go back to the start of this section; were these prophecies deliberately self-fulfilled or manipulated? Was the New Testament deliberately written in a way that would make it consistent with these ancient prophecies? Were they simply too general, maybe even chance happenings, so as to be meaningless? Were these predictions added to the ancient texts after these events occurred, i.e. was there a retrospective update of the Old Testament? I bring these points up because some modern sceptics have done so and also because they are valid questions.

Concerning Self-Fulfilment or Manipulation

It would, firstly, be rather a serious charge to accuse Jesus of lying when he talked about these same prophets on the road to Emmaus after his resurrection, as described in Luke 24:25–27: 'How foolish you are, and how slow to believe all that the prophets have spoken! Did not the Messiah have to suffer these things and then enter his glory?' And beginning with Moses and all the Prophets, he explained to them what was said in all the Scriptures concerning himself.

The above, and other statements by Jesus concerning himself as the fulfilment of ancient prophecy, cannot be ignored, coming from the most righteous one who ever lived, of whom even a Roman centurion said, 'Surely this was a righteous man.' (Luke 23:47.)

Let us first look at this possibility of manipulation. That is, fraudulent activity of some kind in order to somehow prove that Jesus was the Messiah by 'cooking the prophetic books', simply by inserting into the New Testament story certain prophecy fulfilment accounts, whether deliberate, deceptive, through self-fulfilment, or by manipulation. Just a few from the list of Jesus's birth, ministry and death/resurrection should set our minds at rest concerning this. Actually, just a few events should entirely disprove this:

That Jesus would be born of a virgin (Isaiah 7:14; Luke 2:4–6). That Jesus would be born in Bethlehem (Micah 5:2; Luke 2:4–6). Each was outside the control of either Jesus himself or his followers. His birth in Bethlehem was in fact under Roman control and was because of an imperial census. That Jesus would be crucified with criminals (Isaiah 53:12; Matthew 27:38) was another event that was outside the control of either Jesus or his disciples, as would the fact that Jesus's hands and feet would be pierced (Psalm 22:16; John 19:36–37). It was the Roman soldiers who would gamble for Jesus's garments (Psalm 22:18; John 19:23–24). Hopefully, these few out of a larger number should be sufficient to convince us concerning this matter.

Concerning Generality

How about the suggestion that these predictions were too general? Well, many of these were very specific. Indeed, so specific that when reading the above list one could think that they were New Testament texts about Jesus, not Old Testament writings of history in advance, predicting these events some 450 to 1,000 years before they happened. Jesus being born of a virgin could not have been more specific; neither could the birth of Jesus in Bethlehem, the former written many centuries before the birth of Jesus, the latter in 735 to 700 BC. Then there was Jesus's ministry in Galilee; Jesus entering Jerusalem riding on a donkey, Jesus being betrayed for thirty pieces of silver, Jesus crucified with criminals, Jesus's hands and feet being pierced, Roman soldiers gambling over his garments, Jesus being assigned a grave with the wicked and with a rich man in his death (Isaiah 53:9), the rich man widely recognised as referring to the borrowed tomb of Joseph of Arimathea (Matthew 27:57–60). I have not even begun to talk about the key events such as Jesus's crucifixion which, although predicted as early as 1,000 BC in Psalm 22, was in fact only introduced as a capital punishment much later. It was used by the Persians in the sixth century BC and later brought to the Eastern Mediterranean by Alexander the Great in the fourth century BC, and by the Phoenicians to Rome in the third century BC.[3] Neither have I talked about his resurrection or ascension; all were predicted in the Old Testament.

3. *Encyclopaedia Britannica Online*, 'Crucifixion: Capital Punishment'. Accessed on 12 October 2018. https://www.britannica.com/topic/crucifixion-capital-punishment.

Ragnar, 'A Funny Gaffe – Fit for a Good Friday. The Puzzle of Psalm 22' in *Consider the Gospel*, April 2015.

Chapter Nineteen
Four Specific Predictions

I would like to spend a little more time with just four of these predictions, to look further into their truth and specificity.[1] Where would the Messiah be born? What miraculous sign would accompany his birth? What would the Messiah achieve? When would these events happen? That is, to look at the where, the what, the why, and the when.

Where Would the Messiah be Born?

That the Messiah was to be born in Bethlehem was widely understood by the Jewish leaders in their reply to King Herod upon the visit of the Magi, the wise men, as recorded in Matthew's Gospel (Matthew 2:1–12). The prophet Micah, who prophesied from 737 to 696 BC and who wrote the book of Micah, predicted:

> But you, Bethlehem Ephrathah, though you are small among the clans of Judah, out of you will come for me one who will be ruler over Israel, whose origins are from of old, from ancient times.
>
> (Micah 5:2)

1. Dennis Prager and Alfred Kolatch, 'Did Jesus Fulfil Messianic Prophecy?' in *Jews for Jesus*. San Francisco, California, 94102, USA.

> He will stand and shepherd his flock in the strength of the Lord, in the majesty of the name of the Lord his God. And they will live securely, for then his greatness will reach to the ends of the Earth.
>
> (Micah 5:4)

This prophecy clearly points to the Messiah because:

1. Micah was describing a future king of Israel.
2. His kingdom would be worldwide (Micah 5:4).
3. He pre-existed from eternity and was not a created being, indicating his divine nature (Micah 5:2).
4. He would redeem Israel from her enemies.
5. He would establish security and peace for the Jewish people – and he would be born in Bethlehem, logically as this was the home of his human ancestor and of another king, King David.[2]

The addition of Ephrathah was inserted in order to distinguish Bethlehem in the tribe of Judah from another Bethlehem during that time, in the tribe of Zebulun. Thus the possibilities for the Messiah's birth were narrowed down to just one small specific village near Jerusalem and this was predicted seven hundred years before it took place.[3]

The fulfilment of this ancient prophecy of Bethlehem is recorded by three of the New Testament gospel writers: Matthew (2: 1–6); Luke (2:4–5, 7, 15) and John (7:42).

What Miraculous Sign Would Accompany Jesus's birth?

One miraculous sign was that the Messiah would be born of a

2. Prager and Kolatch, 'Did Jesus Fulfil Messianic Prophecy?' in *Jews for Jesus*, p.2

3. George and Ray Konig, *100 Prophecies: Ancient Biblical Prophecies that Foretold the Future.* CreateSpace Independent Publishing Platform, October 2008, p.43.

virgin. This was prophesied by Isaiah, a major prophet who lived in Jerusalem around 735 BC; the same time that he wrote his book which contained many other Messianic prophecies. In this one he wrote:

> Therefore the Lord himself will give you a sign: 'The virgin will conceive and give birth to a son, and will call him Immanuel. 'God is with us.
>
> (Isaiah 7:14)

Isaiah also wrote about the birth of the Messiah and gave us some of his titles:

> For to us a child is born, to us a son is given, and the government will be on his shoulders. And he will be called Wonderful Counselor, Mighty God, Everlasting Father, Prince of Peace. Of the greatness of his government and peace there will be no end. He will reign on David's throne and over his kingdom, establishing and upholding it with justice and righteousness from that time on and forever. The zeal of the Lord Almighty will accomplish this.
>
> (Isaiah 9:6–7)

The fulfilment of the prophecy of the virgin birth can be found in two of the Gospels; those of Matthew (Matthew 1:18–23) and Luke (Luke 1:26–38). Here is Matthew's account:

> This is how the birth of Jesus the Messiah came about: His mother Mary was pledged to be married to Joseph, but before they came together, she was found to be pregnant through the Holy Spirit. Because Joseph her husband was faithful to the law, and yet did not want to expose her to public disgrace, he had in mind to divorce her quietly. But after he had considered this, an angel of the Lord appeared to him in a dream and said, 'Joseph son of David, do not be afraid to take Mary home as your wife, because what is conceived in her is from the Holy Spirit. She will give birth

to a son, and you are to give him the name Jesus, because he will save his people from their sins.' All this took place to fulfil what the Lord had said through the prophet: 'The virgin will conceive and give birth to a son, and they will call him Immanuel' (which means 'God with us').

(Matthew 1: 18–23)

The above-translated word in Isaiah 7:14 for virgin is from the Hebrew word *almah.* The literal translation of *almah* from the original Hebrew means 'maiden' or 'young woman.' However, besides the fact that maidens were both religiously and culturally expected to be virgins until marriage, the word *almah* is used elsewhere in the Bible when referring to virgins. According to one scholarly work,

> There is no instance where it can be proved that *almah* designates a young woman who is not a virgin. The fact of virginity is obvious in Genesis 24:43 where *almah* is used of one who was being sought as a bride for Isaac.[4]

Mary herself, in Luke 1:34, said to the angel, 'How can this be, since I have no relations with a man?' She makes the clear, unambiguous, claim to have been chaste before the conception of Jesus.

What Would the Messiah Achieve?

The Old Testament declares that the Messiah will die as a sin offering. Isaiah declares, in what is known as the great prophecy of the Suffering Servant, in Isaiah 53:

> 'But he was pierced for our transgressions, he was crushed for our iniquities; the punishment that brought us peace was on him, and by his wounds we are healed. We all, like sheep, have gone astray, each of us has turned to our own way; and the Lord has laid on him the iniquity of us all. By oppression

4. Konig, *100 Prophecies*, p.42.

> and judgement he was taken away. Yet who of his generation protested? For he was cut off from the land of the living; for the transgression of my people he was punished. Therefore I will give him a portion among the great, and he will divide the spoils with the strong, because he poured out his life unto death, and was numbered with the transgressors. For he bore the sin of many, and made intercession for the transgressors'.
>
> (Isaiah 53:5–6, 8, 12)

In these verses, Isaiah describes the Messiah as:

1. Rejected by people.
2. Suffering.
3. Wounded for Israel's transgressions.
4. Carrying the guilt of the people upon him.[5]

The Hebrew word *m'cholal* in Isaiah 53:5 means 'to pierce'. That is, Jesus the 'suffering servant' was pierced through. Jesus was the fulfilment of Isaiah's prophecy who would die as a sacrifice to forgive us for our sins. He was revealed to John the Baptist and recorded in the New Testament in John's Gospel as follows:

> The next day John saw Jesus coming toward him and said, 'Look! There is the Lamb of God who takes away the sin of the world!
>
> (John 1:29)

Also, in the book of Acts:

> All the prophets testify about him that everyone who believes in him receives forgiveness of sins through his name.
>
> (Acts 10:43)

5. Prager and Kolatch, 'Did Jesus Fulfil Messianic Prophecy?' in *Jews for Jesus.*

Also in Acts:

> Therefore, my friends, I want you to know that through Jesus the forgiveness of sins is proclaimed to you. Through him everyone who believes is set free from every sin, a justification you were not able to obtain under the law of Moses.
>
> (Acts 13:38–39)

The Old Testament Prophet Zechariah (who wrote between 520–518 BC) predicted that the Messiah would be pierced and that the people of Israel would mourn and weep when they saw him:

> And I will pour out on the house of David and the inhabitants of Jerusalem a spirit of grace and supplication. They will look on me, the one they have pierced, and they will mourn for him as one mourns for an only child, and grieve bitterly for him as one grieves for a first-born son.
>
> (Zechariah 12:10)

The Hebrew phrase *et asher daqru* used in the original of the above means 'whom they have pierced'. The verb refers to piercing and running through with a sharp weapon.[6]

Similarly in Psalm 22:16, 'Dogs surround me, a pack of villains encircles me; they pierce my hands and my feet'.

These predict the crucifixion of Jesus Christ, as does Isaiah 53:5, many centuries before it happened. Christ's crucifixion fulfilment is recorded in the New Testament as follows:

> When they came to the place called the Skull, they crucified him there, along with the criminals – one on his right, the other on his left. Jesus

6. Kevin D. Zuber, 'Daniel 9:24–27, When Will Messiah Come?' in *The Moody Handbook of Messianic Prophecy, Studies and Expositions of the Messiah in the Old Testament*, general editors M. Rydelnik and E. Blum. Moody Publishers, Chicago, 2019.

said, 'Father, forgive them, for they do not know what they are doing.

(Luke 23:33–34a)

In John's gospel he writes:

> Instead, one of the soldiers pierced Jesus's side with a spear, bringing a sudden flow of blood and water.
>
> (John 19:34)

When Would These Events Happen?

The timing and sequence of the coming of Jesus were foretold with great accuracy by the prophet Daniel, who wrote just over six centuries before. This book was completed by 530 BC.[7] Daniel was a great Old Testament prophet who, amongst other things, accurately prophesied the rise of the Medo-Persian, Greek, and Roman empires long before they existed. He foretold the timing of the arrival of the Messiah as follows:

> Know and understand this: From the time the word goes out to restore and rebuild Jerusalem until the Anointed One, the ruler, comes, there will be seven 'sevens,' and sixty-two 'sevens.' It will be rebuilt with streets and a trench, but in times of trouble. After the sixty-two 'sevens', the Anointed One will be put to death and will have nothing. The people of the ruler who will come will destroy the city and the sanctuary.
>
> (Daniel 9:25–26a)

> He will confirm a covenant with many for one 'seven'. In the middle of the 'seven' he will put an end to sacrifice and offering.
>
> (Daniel 9:27a)

7. Arnold Fruchtenbaum, 'The Messianic Time Table According to Daniel the Prophet', *Jews for Jesus*, 20 April 2018.

Daniel's prophecy predicts the following specific timetable of events that would come to pass after Daniel's time:

1. There would be a decree to rebuild Jerusalem.
2. After that, Jerusalem would be rebuilt.
3. The Messiah would arrive after a very specific time period.
4. The Messiah would be cut off (killed).
5. The city (Jerusalem) and the sanctuary (the Temple) would be destroyed. This happened in the year 70 AD.

This is how the timing has been arrived at.[8] In accordance with some Scripture references (e.g. the Old Testament books of Numbers 14:34 and Ezekiel 4:6), one day in the above prophecy is equivalent to one year. It says that these events will occur sixty-nine weeks (seven weeks plus threescore and two weeks = 7 + 62 = 69), that is, sixty-nine units of seven years, or 483 lunar years, as the Jewish calendar is a lunar one, consisting of 360 days, not our solar one of 365 days. So, this prophecy predicts that there will be 483 lunar years (that is, our 476 solar years) from the 'issuance of the word to rebuild Jerusalem' and the coming of the Messiah; then the Messiah will be 'cut off'. The date for the time 'from the going forth of the commandment', was the edict of Artaxerxes (King of Persia) to Nehemiah (the king's cupbearer) which named Jerusalem and authorised the Jewish people to rebuild and restore the city (Nehemiah 6:1–8). This decree, according to historical sources, was given in 444 BC.

8. Prager and Kolatch, 'Did Jesus Fulfil Messianic Prophecy?' in *Jews for Jesus*. Fruchtenbaum, 'The Messianic Time Table' in *Jews for Jesus*.
J. Warner Wallace, 'Perhaps the Greatest Old Testament Prophecy of All', in *Cold Case Christianity*, 8 March 2019.

Jesus of Nazareth undoubtedly fulfils Daniel's passage. Daniel's prophecy is very clear about the following:

First, the Messiah was to be on Earth 483 years after the decree was issued to rebuild Jerusalem, given in 444 BC.

Second, after his appearance on Earth, he was to be killed.

Third, the death of the Messiah had to come sometime before the destruction of Jerusalem and the temple, which occurred in the year 70 AD.[9]

Additionally, in the midst of the week when the Messiah was put to death, Daniel prophesies 'in the middle of the "seven" he will put an end to sacrifice and offering'. (Daniel 9:27a.) This refers to when the veil in the temple was torn; this event shows that sacrifice and offering were from then on no longer needed, as Jesus had once and for all given his perfect sacrifice.[10] The temple veil being torn is referred to in three of the gospels (Matthew 27:51; Mark 15:38, and Luke 23:45) and marks the abolition of the need for the sacrificial system, having been fulfilled by the sacrificial death of Jesus Christ.

From the Hebrew Bible, the Old Testament, which is known and proven to have been written long before the time of Jesus (see the Dead Sea Scrolls in chapter twenty for further evidence), we have examined in some detail four key prophecies concerning the promised Messiah:

1. He would be born in Bethlehem.
2. He would be born of a virgin.
3. He would suffer and die to pay the penalty for our sin.
4. The timing of when he would die, which resulted in the temple veil being torn in two and with the ending of the need for the sacrificial system (estimated to be in 30 AD), then after his death, Jerusalem and the Temple would be destroyed (in 70 AD).

9. Fruchtenbaum, 'The Messianic Time Table' in *Jews for Jesus*.

10. Prager and Kolatch, 'Did Jesus Fulfil Messianic Prophecy?' in *Jews for Jesus*.

Chapter Twenty
The Dead Sea Scrolls

My last question examining the authenticity of the fulfilment of these prophecies is as follows: were these predictions added to the ancient texts after these events occurred? Let us now look at the evidence from the Dead Sea Scrolls.

I start with a story from the twentieth century, so remarkable that any work of fiction would find it difficult to compete. In 1947 a young Bedouin shepherd by the name of Muhammad Ahmed el-Dhib, with others, was tending his sheep and goats on the shore of the Dead Sea in the Judean desert, near the ancient site of Qumran.[1] He was searching for a lost goat and came across a cave with a small opening. In the belief that his goat may somehow have fallen into the cave, Muhammad threw some stones into the opening. What he heard was the noise of breaking clay pottery. He and his companions later climbed down into the cave and found a number of clay jars, seven of which contained leather and papyrus scrolls. Later on, Muhammed took these scrolls to a cobbler and antiquities dealer in Bethlehem named Khando. Khando in turn passed them to a Syrian Orthodox archbishop named Mar (Athanasius) Samuel. He knew that these scrolls were written in Hebrew and suspected that they were very old and valuable. Further experts were contacted, and in due course, it was found that the texts were more than two

1. Patrick Zukeran, *The Dead Sea Scrolls Shed Light on the Accuracy of Our Bible.* Probe Ministries, April 2006.

thousand years old. Later, between 1952 and 1956, archaeologists searched other caves in the same region. Altogether, they discovered nearly 1,100 ancient documents and more than 100,000 fragments, from eleven nearby caves. Thus was discovered one of the greatest archaeological finds of the twentieth century, now widely known as the Dead Sea Scrolls. Our thanks go to Muhammed for losing his goat and for making this discovery, to Khando who could easily have made them into pairs of sandals but didn't, and to various experts who understood their significance!

Many of the Dead Sea Scrolls contained biblical texts. Fragments were found from every book of the Old Testament, except for the book of Esther. There was also a complete book of Isaiah, with this particular scroll being dated to around 100 BC. Besides biblical texts, the scrolls included many other documents, including other religious writings outside of the Hebrew Bible. Most of these scrolls are in Hebrew, but some are in Aramaic, others in Greek. These scrolls were hidden by the Essenes, a now extinct sect of the Jewish nation, to protect them. The writing of the Dead Sea Scrolls was accurately dated by three dating methods, including carbon-14 dating, and the dates arrived at were very similar: some documents were written as early as the third century BC, others up to the first century AD, depending upon the document written. These scrolls, mostly written before the time of Jesus, were themselves copied from far earlier sacred writings which the Essenes would have had access to.

What is the significance of the Dead Sea Scrolls? One answer is that they play a crucial role in assessing the accurate preservation of the Old Testament writings. Thus detailed comparisons can be made between these early writings and those of more recent texts. Our current Old Testament is translated from what is called the Masoretic Text. This, for example, is what the Institute for Bible

Translation's Old Testament translations are mostly based upon. Before the discovery of these scrolls in 1947, the oldest surviving Hebrew text of the Old Testament was the Masoretic Aleppo Codex, which is dated to 935 AD. The Dead Sea Scrolls now give us manuscripts that pre-date this by a thousand years! How similar are these to the Masoretic text? There have been decades of very careful study, with the conclusive answer that these scrolls are almost identical to that of the Masoretic text. The distinguished Hebrew scholar Millar Burrows has written:

> It is a matter of wonder that through something like one thousand years the text underwent so little alteration. As I said in my first article on the scroll, 'Herein lies its chief importance, supporting the fidelity of the Masoretic tradition'.[2]

A separate comparative study was undertaken with the Isaiah scroll, written by the Essenes around 100 BC but based upon the far earlier original Hebrew text, completed by 450 BC.[3] After a lot of work, the Dead Sea and Masoretic Isaiah texts were found to be virtually identical. There were only some minor spelling mistakes, but none affected the meaning of the text. We can now say with certainty that the Old Testament has been accurately and carefully preserved. The Jewish scribes, over many centuries, were very careful, faithful, and successful in copying these early texts.[4]

2. Millar Burrows, *The Dead Sea Scrolls*. Viking Press, New York, 1955, p.304. Quoted in Norman Geisler and William Nix, *General Introduction to the Bible*. Moody Press, Chicago, 1986, p.367.

3. Zukeran, *The Dead Sea Scrolls*.

4. Jeff A. Benner, *The Great Isaiah Scroll and the Masoretic Text*. Ancient Hebrew Research Center.

The Scrolls and Old Testament Messianic Prophecy

There are many prophecies in the Old Testament concerning the coming of Jesus Christ. These were made centuries before the birth of Christ and were both specific and detailed in content. We have strong evidence that the Old Testament, written in Hebrew, was completed by 450 BC.[5] The Greek translation of the Old Testament is called the Septuagint; it was written around 250 BC, during the reign of Egyptian pharaoh Ptolemy Philadelphus who ruled from 285 to 246 BC.[6] The Dead Sea Scrolls provide further evidence that the Old Testament existed well before the time of Christ, with portions from the book of Samuel being found to date from the third century BC. Some fragments from Daniel date to the second century BC and the Isaiah scroll to around 100 BC.[7] So, the many prophecies about Christ in the Old Testament pre-dated his birth and we can say with certainty that they were not tampered with in any way after his coming.

Four Kinds of New Testament Interpretations of Old Testament Prophecy

How did the New Testament writers interpret the Hebrew Bible, our Old Testament, to reveal that Jesus was the fulfilment of the messianic hope? This can be demonstrated by looking at Matthew, whose primary intention was to convince the Jews (who really knew their Bible) that Jesus was the promised Messiah, in his second chapter. Briefly, he does this in four ways: direct fulfilment, summary fulfilment, typical fulfilment, and applicational fulfilment.[8]

5. Zukeran, *The Dead Sea Scrolls.*

6. Zukeran, *The Dead Sea Scrolls.*

7. Zukeran, *The Dead Sea Scrolls.*

8. Michael A. Rydelnik, 'The Old Testament in the New Testament' in *The Moody Handbook of Messianic Prophecy, Studies and Expositions of the Messiah in the Old Testament*, general editors M. Rydelnik and E. Blum. Moody Publishers, Chicago, 2019.

The first method was the simple expression of direct fulfilment, where in Matthew 2:2 he writes that the wise men from the East asked 'where is he who has been born King of the Jews?' to which the direct reply from the Jewish scholars was the citation directly to Bethlehem, as predicted in Micah 5:2. A basic record in Micah prophesied that the Messiah would be born in Bethlehem, and it has happened.

The second method, summary fulfilment, can be seen in Matthew chapter two, where it states that Joseph returned to his hometown of Nazareth, and this was 'to fulfil what was spoken through the prophets, that he will be called a Nazarene' (Matthew 2:23). Nowhere in the Hebrew Bible, however, does it say that 'he will be called a Nazarene!' So, how do we explain this? This verse is often used by sceptics to 'prove' that Matthew was making things up or something similar, which is the reason why I am including this section. For those with some Scriptural knowledge, which most certainly would have included the Jews at the time of Jesus, a relatively simple interpretation of 'he will be called a Nazarene' would have been that this was a summary of the teaching from the prophets about the Messiah. The text in Matthew supports this as, here alone, Matthew states that this fulfils the words of the 'prophets' (plural), referring to many prophecies and not just one. The theme that Matthew is summarising is that 'Nazarene' was a term of derision and Matthew is summarising the Old Testament teaching that the Messiah would be despised.

Other examples showing that this was a disparaging term can be seen in two other passages of Scripture, e.g. John 7:41–42, 52 and Matthew 26:71. These references are in agreement with other passages of the Old Testament which indicate that the Messiah would be despised. Examples of this are found in Psalms 22 and 69; Zechariah 11:4–14 and Isaiah 50 and 53. Matthew summarises all these ancient predictions from prophecy in the single phrase 'He shall be called a Nazarene'.[9] In addition to direct and summary fulfilment, the two other kinds of fulfilment which Matthew uses to convince his knowledgeable Jewish readers are what are known as typical and applicational fulfilment; examples of which can also both be found in Matthew chapter two.

Briefly, a definition of typical fulfilment is 'the recognition of a correspondence between New and Old Testaments, based on a conviction of the unchanging character of the principles of God's working' (Matthew 2:15 and its comparison with Hosea 11:1 would be a good example).[10] Without going too deeply into this, Matthew's use of this technique showed a deep knowledge of the Scriptures, using a well-established method in the Old Testament and which would have been more than sufficient to convince his knowledgeable Jewish readers.

Finally, applicational fulfilment can be seen in Matthew 2:16–18 when he is citing Jeremiah 31:15. This last category is the application of an Old Testament prophecy to a similar situation in the New Testament era. In this particular case, just as Rachel represented Jewish mothers who wept at the death and exile of their sons, Jewish mothers once again mourned when Herod murdered their children. So, New Testament authors not only cited the direct fulfilments of Messianic prophecies – which I have based the vast majority of this chapter on – they also included summary, typical, and applicational fulfilments.[11]

To conclude this section; it has been well stated by Sailhamer

9. Michael A. Rydelnik, 'The Old Testament in the New Testament' in *The Moody Handbook of Messianic Prophecy*.

10. Michael A. Rydelnik, 'The Old Testament in the New Testament' in *The Moody Handbook of Messianic Prophecy*.

11. Michael A. Rydelnik, 'The Old Testament in the New Testament' in *The Moody Handbook of Messianic Prophecy*.

as follows: 'I believe the messianic thrust of the Old Testament was the *whole* reason why the books of the Hebrew Bible were written.'[12] In other words, the Hebrew Bible was not written as the national literature of Israel. Also, it was probably not written to the nation of Israel as such. Rather, it was written as the expression of the deep-seated messianic hope of a small group of faithful prophets and their followers. I might also add to those great words: the wonderful thing is that what they wrote all those centuries before actually came to pass!

12. John H. Sailhamer, 'Messiah and the Hebrew Bible' in *The Moody Handbook of Messianic Prophecy, Studies and Expositions of the Messiah in the Old Testament*, general editors M. Rydelnik and E. Blum. Moody Publishers, Chicago, 2019.

PART FOUR

APOLOGETIC EVIDENCE
Science and God

Chapter Twenty-One
Famous Scientists and Christians

Science is obviously a vast area, with many books and immense thought contributed by scientists, many of whom are also Christians. I have been a biological scientist all my working life, and I wish to pay my deep respects to all those with much greater minds than mine who have focused on this area. This chapter is just to explain my own thoughts around this, not least out of personal integrity. The main intention of writing this book has been to explain my own story, and how, unexpectedly, I entered into a personal relationship with God through the blood and atoning sacrifice of Jesus Christ. This life of living out the Holy Spirit's work within, and the Christian journey has been so powerful for me, that there is a slight feeling of 'red herring' around this huge subject of science in relation to God. In particular, the erroneous public view that science and Christianity are in conflict has been mercilessly promulgated by those with an atheistic agenda; one fairly recent example being that of Dr Richard Dawkins.

The truth, however, is that a very large number of scientists have been Christians in the past, as well as in the present. This stated or implied 'conflict' between science and religion is a modern invention and is illusory. I would even go so far as to say that a large number of scientists are both giants of the Christian faith as well as giants in their chosen fields, with scientific discovery being part of their worship of God as they delight in unravelling the ways in which

God has created his world. It is also the case that these scientists have correctly understood that God himself delights in and gives us his help as we work to unravel what God has already done in creation. In that process we can make good use of many discoveries which enable us to help others in major ways. Advances in medicine and in agriculture are two major fields where this has happened. It seems to be both God's delight as well as ours that there is this divine–human partnership.

Famous Scientists and their Beliefs: Nobel Prize Winners

To counter the current false impression in the public arena that science has now replaced religion as the only reasonable way of looking at the world, the fact is that over 65 per cent of Nobel Laureates between 1901 and 2000 identified themselves as Christians. A further 20 per cent were Jewish and 1 per cent were Muslim.[1] Christians have made up 64 per cent of the physics awards, 65 per cent of medicine, and 74 per cent of the chemistry. Atheists comprised only 5 per cent, 9 per cent and 7 per cent respectively in the above scientific disciplines, a remarkably small percentage. This provides some evidence that science and belief in God are not in opposition and that, during this period at least, many of the most eminent scientists in the world have believed in God, in contrast to what is perceived as the popular view.

Famous Scientists in History, Famous Scientists in the Present

There were, and are, many. One outstanding scientist and Christian was Johannes Kepler, who was born in Weil der Stadt, Germany, in December 1571. He is best known for his laws of planetary motion

1. Baruch A. Shalev, *100 Years of Nobel Prizes*. Americas Group Publications, 2002.

and for writing several books which provided a key basis for Newton's theory of universal gravitation. Kepler, despite his great achievements, was a humble Christian man. He was able to say 'Let my name perish if only the name of God the Father is thereby elevated.' Another saying attributed to him was 'I am merely thinking God's thoughts after him.' And again, he was able to say towards the end of his life 'I had the intention of becoming a theologian . . . But now I see God is, by my endeavours, also glorified in astronomy, for "the heavens declare the glory of God".'

Another outstanding scientist was Sir Francis Bacon, who was born in London in January 1561. Bacon was a devout Christian, and he introduced what is known as the scientific (or investigative) method, where scientific laws are discovered by the harnessing and analysis of information from experiments and observations, in contrast to the use of arguments based on logic. He viewed science as a way to learn deeper truths about God. In a key work published in 1623, he wrote 'a little knowledge makes men atheists, but a more thorough acquaintance with the sciences brings them back again to religion.' He was also a statesman, serving as attorney general and Lord Chancellor of England.

Galileo (Galileo Galilei), who was born in Pisa, Italy, in February 1564, was one of the most famous scientists who ever lived. He is considered the father of modern astronomy, the father of modern physics, and the father of modern science. His achievements are far too many to list here, but he made major contributions to maths, physics, and astronomy. For example, his improvements to the telescope were then used to confirm the phases of Venus, the discovery of the four largest moons of Jupiter, and the observation and analysis of sunspots. His work on proving that the sun rather than the Earth is at the centre of our solar system brought him into conflict with the then Catholic Church. He has been called the father of modern science by Albert Einstein, Stephen Hawking, and many others. He remained a devout Christian throughout his life and saw science and religion as being interrelated. For example, he stated that 'God is known by nature in his works, and by doctrine in his revealed word,' and that 'the Bible teaches men how to go to heaven, not how the heavens go.'

Sir Isaac Newton, who was born in Lincolnshire in December 1642, is also regarded as one of the greatest scientists who ever lived. He was a mathematician, physicist, astronomer, and theologian and became the Lucasian Professor of Mathematics at Cambridge University (as more recently did Stephen Hawking). Besides his work on universal gravitation, Newton discovered the three laws of motion which comprise the basis of modern physics. He discovered calculus which led to powerful ways of solving mathematical problems. He was the father of optics and his study of white light led to the discovery of the colour spectrum. His book *Principia Mathematica* is widely perceived as the greatest scientific book ever written. Newton was a firm believer in God, although he held some unorthodox views. He wrote, 'Gravity explains the motions of the planets, but it cannot explain who set the planets in motion.' He also wrote, 'God governs all things, and knows all that is or can be done.'

Carl Linnaeus was yet another scientist who saw no conflict between science and Christian belief but, rather, central to it. He was born in May 1707 within the Almhult Municipality, in southern Sweden. He was a botanist, zoologist, and physician and is known as the father of modern taxonomy, which is the system for classifying and naming organisms. This is how we now have in nature the grouping of organisms into species, genus, family, order, class, phylum, kingdom and domain. Linnaeus became the professor of medicine and botany at Uppsala University. He wrote 'the study of nature would reveal the divine order of God's creation, and it was the naturalist's task to construct a "natural classification" that would reveal this order in the universe.'

Robert Boyle, born in January 1627 in Lismore, Ireland, is widely regarded as a key founder of modern chemistry. All students of chemistry will have heard of him, as it was he who discovered that the volume of a gas decreases with increasing pressure and vice versa, within a closed system. This is known as the famous Boyle's Law. He was a devout Christian and writer of theology. He considered science and Scripture to exist in harmony and that conflicts between science and the Bible were either due to a mistake in science or to an incorrect interpretation of Scripture. In 1681 he wrote a theological work *A Discourse of Things Above Reason*. Boyle promoted Christianity in the East by financially supporting missionaries and Bible translations. In his will, he endowed a series of annual lectures in defence of Christianity. These Boyle Lectures are still held annually in London to this day.

Michael Faraday, born in September 1791 in Southwark, became the first Fullerian Professor of Chemistry at the Royal Institution. He was one of the greatest scientists in history. He discovered the principles behind electromagnetic induction and electrolysis. His discoveries formed the basis of electric motor technology, and it was because of his work that electricity came into practical use. In addition to his great contribution to physics, he was also a great chemist, for example discovering benzene, the system of oxidation numbers, and establishing the terminology of anode, cathode, electrode, and ion. Faraday was a devout Christian and served as an elder in his church. He considered Christianity to be a revelation and that this revelation is found in the Bible. He had a strong sense of the unity of God and nature, which was apparent in both Faraday's personal life and in his work.

Louis Pasteur was born in December 1822 in Dole, France. He discovered the principles of vaccination, fermentation, and pasteurisation, the latter named after him. He demonstrated that microorganisms cause disease and developed the first vaccines against fowl cholera, anthrax, and rabies. He remained a Christian throughout his life and he prayed while he worked. He said, 'posterity will one day laugh at the foolishness of modern philosophers. The more I study nature, the more I stand amazed at the work of the creator. I pray while I am engaged at my work in the laboratory.'

Charles Babbage, born in December 1791 in London, was the first person to create a digital mechanical computer and is known as the 'father of the computer'. His mechanical computer led in due course to more complex designs, but these adhered to the principles that Babbage formulated. He also invented the modern postal system and speedometers. He was a sincere Christian and according to Buxton, his biographer:

> [He] came to believe that the scientific method pursued to its uttermost limit was entirely compatible with revealed religion and he wrote his treatise (called the Ninth Bridgewater Treatise) to prove the point . . .
>
> . . . Babbage believed that the study of the works of nature with scientific precision, was a necessary and indispensable preparation to the understanding and interpreting their testimony of the wisdom and goodness of their divine author.

William Thomson (Lord Kelvin), born in June 1824 in Belfast, Ireland, was a mathematical physicist and engineer. He was the professor of natural philosophy at Glasgow University for over fifty years. He did important work in the mathematical analysis of electricity and in the first and second laws of thermodynamics. He did much to develop modern physics. He invented the electric telegraph and did much else besides. He studied absolute zero temperature and found its correct value. Absolute temperatures are stated in units of Kelvin, in his honour. Thomson kept a strong and simple Christian faith, which included a faithful study of the Bible. His Christian faith permeated his work. For example, he always began his college classes with prayer and regarded his scientific work as an act of worship. He treated science with reverence, 'for a close observation of the phenomena of nature brought one closer to understanding God's works: if you think strongly enough, you will be forced by science to a belief in God, which is the foundation of all religion.' He believed that study of the scientific laws was the noblest privilege granted to man's intelligence.

Chapter Twenty-Two
The Big Bang

When I was at school in the early 1960s there was still some debate as to whether scientists thought that the universe had always existed: that is, what is known as the Steady State theory, or could it be found or proved at the scientific level that a Big Bang or creation event had occurred? I remember thinking at the time, 'If they do discover that the universe had a beginning, then that will indicate that God exists!' The Big Bang was later (in 1964) proved to have occurred, but it was an even greater discovery than was previously expected, in that it was found to be the beginning not just of space, but also of time (space-time). So, time itself began at the creation, in addition to the universe itself. So, as Michael Poole explains:

> The idea that time is part of the creation is very difficult to grasp. But it is similar to the view that St Augustine (of Hippo) held, back in the fourth century. Realising that the Bible teaches that God transcends time, he said that creation was 'with time,' not 'in time.'[1]

Thus the Bible's opening words in Genesis chapter one: 'In the beginning, God created the heavens and the Earth' suggests both the start of time itself, as well as the start of the universe. I also agree with Poole that we cannot prove scientifically whether or not God

1. Michael Poole, *God and the Big Bang – and Other Arguments About Science and Faith*. Christian Publicity Organisation, West Sussex, UK.

exists, simply because science itself is the study of the natural world, of nature. Questions about God are questions about whether there is anything other than nature. So, it is of no use going to science, the study of nature, to find out whether there is anything other than nature! Simply, science just cannot answer questions like this.[2] However, although science can never 'prove' God's existence, it will always be consistent with it, as the earlier scientists in our history understood. As Galileo said, 'God is known by nature in his works, and by doctrine in his revealed word,' and that the 'Bible teaches men how to go to heaven, not how the heavens go.'

2. Poole, *God and the Big Bang*.

Chapter Twenty-Three
Fine-Tuning of the Universe and Planet Earth

In addition to the Big Bang, we have within the past fifty years understood much more clearly the extraordinary fine-tuning of the universe. This has been termed the Goldilocks Principle.[1] In 'Goldilocks and the Three Bears', Goldilocks tastes three different bowls of porridge and finds that only one bowl has 'just the right' temperature, neither too hot nor too cold. In an analogous way, conditions within the universe have been found to be 'just right' for life to exist and thrive. As Professor Stephen Hawking put it, 'like Goldilocks, the development of intelligent life requires that planetary temperatures be "just right".'[2] There are several widely accepted 'Cosmic Constants' which give us some idea of this 'fine-tuning'. Here are a few:

GRAVITATIONAL FORCE CONSTANT: this is the large attractive force that holds people on Earth and enables planets, stars and galaxies to be held together. When measured against the strength of electromagnetism, it seems fine-tuned for life. If gravity had been absent or much weaker, then planets and stars would not have formed. Even if only slightly weaker, then the sun would have been colder. If, on the other hand, gravity had been just a little

1. Father Frank O'Dea, 'Our Goldilocks Universe', in Eucharist: the Basic Spirituality, https://theeucharist.wordpress.com/our-goldilocks-universe/

2. S. Hawking and L. Mlodinow, *The Grand Design*. Bantam Press, 2010.

stronger, then stars would have been much smaller and would have burned up too quickly.[3]

STRONG NUCLEAR FORCE CONSTANT: this is the small-scale attractive force that holds the nuclei of atoms together; otherwise they would repulse each other because of the electromagnetic force. When measured against the electromagnetic force, it seems fine-tuned for life, as for gravity. A significant increase in this attractive force would have resulted in virtually all hydrogen being burned up in the early universe, whereas a significant decrease would have resulted in the universe having fewer stable chemical elements and eliminating several that are essential to life, including carbon and oxygen.

WEAK NUCLEAR FORCE CONSTANT: this governs radioactive decay and its strength and, yet again, seems to be fine-tuned for life to exist. If it were much weaker, then there would have been many more neutrons in the early universe, quickly leading to deuterium and tritium, and to helium. In that case, our life-essential sun (and similarly, other long-lived stars), which depends on hydrogen so that it can burn to helium, would not exist.

COSMOLOGICAL CONSTANT: this controls the expansion speed of the universe, and is the balance between the force of attraction from gravity and the large-scale force of repulsion from space. In reality, these two forces are almost evenly balanced and so this constant is almost zero. If very slightly less in equilibrium, then either the universe would fly apart or the universe would collapse on itself.

3. Jay W. Richards, *List of Fine-Tuning Parameters*. Center for Science and Culture, Discovery Institute, 2020, p283–290.

Simon Friederich, 'Fine-Tuning', The Stanford Encyclopaedia of Philosophy. Last modified 12 November 2021, https://plato.stanford.edu/entries/fine-tuning/

It is estimated that the cosmological constant is fine-tuned to just 1 part in 10 to the power of 120, indeed far less than finding the proverbial 'needle in a haystack.'

There are many other facts of nature that exhibit fine-tuning, without which life would simply not have begun. One is the ratio of masses for protons and electrons within the atom. If protons would be just 0.2 percent heavier, then they would decay into neutrons and destabilise atoms so that, for example, the building blocks for life such as DNA could not be formed.[4] Another is the mass excess of the neutron to the proton. If it was slightly greater than it is (even by a seventh of one percent), then there would be too few heavy elements for life and most of the stars would not exist. If the neutron mass was 0.085 per cent less than it is, then stars would quickly collapse as neutron stars or black holes, so that the universe would simply be full of neutrons and nothing else. There is no inherent reason why protons and neutrons should have these masses.[5]

On Earth itself, we also have evidence of this fine-tuning which enables life to occur, but which can be described as 'local' in contrast to 'cosmic'. There are many such examples. Jay Richards identifies twelve broad factors which are needed to build a habitable planet like ours, but recognises that there are probably many more.[6] Here are some of these:

Having a large moon with the right planetary rotation period stabilises Earth's tilt and contributes to tides. In Earth's case, our moon's gravity stabilises the angle of our planet's axis at a constant 23.5 degrees, thus ensuring fairly temperate seasonal

4. S. Hawking and L. Mlodinow, *The Grand Design*, p.160.

5. D. Couchman, 'The Mass of the Proton and the Neutron as an Example of Fine Tuning For Life in God'. *New Evidence*, May 2011. http://www.focus.org.uk/proton_neutron.php

6. Jay W. Richards, *List of Fine-Tuning Parameters. https://www.discovery.org/m/2020/06/Fine-Tuning-Parameters-Jay-Richards.pdf*

changes and the only climate in our solar system mild enough to sustain complex biological life.

Another one is Earth having just the right mass. A smaller Earth would result in a weaker magnetic field so that the solar wind would strip away our atmosphere, transforming our planet into a dead, barren planet like others in our solar system.

Another is our closeness to the sun. If Earth was only 5 per cent closer to the sun, then it would end up like Venus, with temperatures rising to nearly 500 degrees Celsius. Conversely, if only about 20% further from the sun, then Earth would be far too cold and would be sterile.

Yet another example of fine-tuning is that Earth is protected by the gravitational pulls of Jupiter and Saturn, which protects Earth from too many comet bombardments. Without the protection of these two very large planets, Earth would be far more susceptible to collision from such destructive comets. There are many other factors that help to keep our planet safe and habitable, but the above provides some key examples.

This is what Charles Townes, a Nobel laureate in physics and a Christian, said:

> This is a very special universe: it's remarkable that it came out just this way. If the laws of physics weren't just the way they are, we couldn't be here at all. The sun couldn't be there, the laws of gravity and nuclear laws and magnetic theory, quantum mechanics, and so on, have to be just the way they are for us to be here.[7]

He also said the following concerning the concept of a multiverse,

7. B. A. Powell, 'Explore As Much As We Can': Nobel Prize Winner Charles Townes on Evolution, Intelligent Design, and the Meaning of Life', UC Berkeley News. Last modified 17 June 2005. https://newsarchive.berkeley.edu/news/media/releases/2005/06/17_townes.shtml

which has been much discussed in recent years as an explanation by some for this fine-tuning, rather than God:

> Some scientists argue that 'well, there's an enormous number of universes and each one is a little different. This one just happened to turn out right.' Well, that's a postulate, and it's a pretty fantastic postulate – it assumes there really are an enormous number of universes and that the laws could be different for each of them. The other possibility is that ours was planned, and that's why it has come out so especially.

Prof. George Ellis wrote the following in the scientific journal *Nature* as part of his review of a book about the multiverse concept called *The Hidden Reality* by Brian Greene:

> The multiverse argument is a well-founded philosophical proposal but, as it cannot be tested, it does not belong fully in the scientific fold. Read *The Hidden Reality* with enjoyment, but beware of its misleading title. Greene is not presenting aspects of a known reality; he is telling of unproven theoretical possibilities.[8]

To conclude this chapter, one key question to consider, in view of our world being very special, is does this provide evidence that God exists? After all, we now know that the universe has recently been proven scientifically to have had a beginning but which the Bible, in the book of Genesis, had already proclaimed loudly and clearly several thousand years ago; we have also recently understood scientifically the extraordinary fine-tuning of the universe and Earth, at the cosmic and local level. So, although God's existence cannot be proven at the scientific level simply because this approach

8. George Ellis, 'Cosmology: The Untestable Multiverse', *Nature*. Vol. 469, 2011, p.294–95.

is limited to studying the natural world, the Bible makes it clear that God has revealed himself through what he has made. The following has been wisely said:

> Everything, whether we're talking about the human body in all its complexity, our innate sense of right and wrong, the awe-inspiring power of Niagara Falls, or the wondrous beauty of distant galaxies; everything in the universe tells us *something* about God's power and wisdom.[9]

The Bible proclaims that creation itself provides us all with a clear understanding of God's existence. St Paul wrote that

> God's invisible attributes . . . his eternal power and divine nature, have been clearly seen since the creation of the world, being understood through what he has made.
>
> (Romans 1:20)

and the Psalmist wrote,

> the heavens declare the glory of God, and the expanse proclaims the work of his hand.
>
> (Psalm 19:1–2)

In addition to God's revelation of himself through nature or his creation, the Bible also declares that God has revealed himself to humanity in three further ways. One is via our conscience, our innate sense of right or wrong, with all societies having been found to have a moral code so that for example stealing, lying, or murder is universally condemned. That is, our own sense of right or wrong

9. Aaron Armstrong, 'Does God Make Himself Known?' The Gospel Project. Accessed 7 August 2019, https://gospelproject.lifeway.com/does-god-make-himself-known/

points to God's existence (Romans 2:14–15); the Bible also declares a third way in which God has revealed himself to the world, namely through the person of Jesus Christ (Hebrews 1:1–2). Jesus said that he had come to Earth to reveal the will of God the Father (Matthew 11:27), and the fourth revelation of God is through the Bible itself. The Bible proclaims that it is God's revelation of himself to human beings. It says of itself,

> All Scripture is given by inspiration of God, and is profitable for doctrine, for reproof, for correction, for instruction in righteousness.
>
> (2 Timothy 3:16)

The Bible is our source for knowing God and his plan for us.[10]

10. D. Stewart, 'How Has God Revealed Himself To Humanity?' Blue Letter Bible, https://www.blueletterbible.org/faq/don_stewart/don_stewart_293.cfm

Chapter Twenty-Four
Evolution and Natural Selection

When I was first taught Darwin's theory of evolution in school at the age of sixteen, my biology master wisely did not bring religion into it. That was helpful, as we were able to see the evidence in its own right, on its own terms, without being influenced by philosophical or other matters. Evolution, in its strict biological sense, is accepted by virtually all biological and other scientists, including by 97 per cent of all US scientists in a 2009 survey.[1] The same view is held by such renowned UK scientific bodies as the Royal Society and the Geological Society of London. This has been the case for well over a hundred years. It provides the 'backbone' for several of the sciences, including biology, geology, and geography, and is not in dispute by those working in these areas.

Evolution is of particular interest to me, not least because I worked for my biological PhD at a world-renowned plant breeding institution, where in effect we were speeding up the evolutionary process by employing artificial selection to create crops with improved yield, quality, and other beneficial traits. Farmers have been using selective breeding for many hundreds of years, both of plants and animals. Artificial selection works in a similar way to natural selection, except that the decisions are made by human

1. 'Section 5: Evolution, Climate Change and Other Issues'. Pew Research Centre, accessed 9 July 2009, https://www.pewresearch.org/politics/2009/07/09/section-5-evolution-climate-change-and-other-issues/

interference, not by nature. As a former colleague quipped, 'We are crossing the best with the best, and hoping for the best!' In reality, we worked with great precision, employing the latest genetic tools and statistical methodology, and were successful in producing much improved varieties of grasses, clovers, cereals, and other crops.[2]

One way of understanding evolution is to look at relationships between different organisms, including those of humans. The Swedish biologist Carl Linnaeus (1707–78) introduced the science of taxonomy, the classification of organisms based upon their similarities: initially, their morphology or structure. For example, his original classification scheme for plants was based upon their sexual structure, with plants organised on the basis of the number, size, and method of their male parts, their stamens, and upon their female parts, their pistils.[3] In his *Systema Naturea*, published in 1735, and in his future works, he divided organisms into distinct taxonomic categories: domain, kingdom, phylum, class, order, family, genus, and species.

An example of taxonomic classification can be given for the domestic cat: *Felis catus*.[4] As a member of the genus *Felis*, one of our favourite pets is closely related to jungle cats and wild cats; in turn, as a member of the family Felidae, it is also more distantly related to cheetahs, lions, tigers and leopards; then, as a member of the order Carnivora, it is even more distantly related to bears, raccoons, badgers, weasels and skunks; then as a member of the class Mammalia (mammals), which produce fur, milk and look

2. Aberystwyth University, '100 Years of Plant Breeding'. https://www.aber.ac.uk/en/ibers/about-us/history/100-years-of-plant-breeding/

3. Marta Paterlini, 'There Shall Be Order: The Legacy of Linnaeus in the Age of Molecular Biology', EMBO Reports (2007) 8, Oxford, p 814–16.

4. '*Felis catus*', ITIS (Integrated Taxonomic Information System - Report) accessed 26 February 2021, https://www.itis.gov/servlet/SingleRpt/SingleRpt?search_topic=TSN&search_value=183798#null

after their young, they are further distantly related to rats, mice, kangaroos, whales, dolphins, and sheep.

Since Linnaeus's classification of organisms based upon their similarities, it has become increasingly evident that all living things on Earth are biologically related to one another. Through careful analyses, biologists have been able to build up trees of life, with similar organisms placed closely together on the same branches and more distantly related ones placed further apart.

Molecular family trees, analogous to human family genealogy, have now been built up for relationships between organisms. Fairly recent molecular examples (from work that began in Cambridge in 1959) have included the construction of the family trees of the proteins myoglobin and haemoglobin, found in almost every multi-celled animal and involved with oxygen in the blood.[5] Their differing molecular structures have now been compared across a wide range of mammals, birds, reptiles, amphibians, fish, worms and molluscs. These structural similarities and differences have been used to create a family tree of globin variation and, crucially, these molecular family trees have been found to match those earlier family trees based on their anatomical similarities. That is, they have been found to be one and the same, and to be in entire agreement with the pre-existing Darwinian anatomical and fossil evidence of common descent concerning these organisms.

More recently, family trees have also now been produced for other proteins such as cytochrome c, which serves a vital function in respiration within cells, and for the proteins trypsin and chymotrypsin, involved with protein digestion. Again, all these point to the same two conclusions, namely the inter-relatedness

5. National Academy of Sciences, 'Evidence Supporting Biological Evolution', in *Science and Creationism: A View from the National Academy of Sciences*. National Academies Press, 2nd revised edition, 1999.

of all biological organisms, and their common descent from older, simpler organisms.

The newer field of genomics has, over recent years, provided even further compelling evidence for biological evolution that removes any possibility of doubt. We will consider this a little further on, but let us first examine the robust textbook evidence steadily built up before, during and after the time of Charles Darwin, who published his book *The Origin of Species* in 1859. This textbook evidence was before the recent convincing molecular evidence as outlined above and the even more recent genomic evidence described below, and can broadly be divided into fossil evidence, comparative anatomy, embryology, and biogeography.

Fossils began to be studied long before Darwin's work on evolution in the 1800s. In fact, they started to be carefully studied in the 1600s.[6] It was realised during this much earlier time that, as much later with evolution, organisms had changed systematically over very long periods of time. Fossils are mainly found in sedimentary rocks, formed when mineral and organic material is laid down and forms layers or strata. This process normally takes millions of years. Younger strata are formed above older strata, in discrete layers, a process known as superposition. It is well documented that the fossils found in the lower, older strata are more primitive than the ones found higher up, in the newer strata.[7] Thus, for example: 'trilobites are found in the lower, older layers; giant insects and ferns are found higher up in the younger layers, and dinosaurs higher again, in even younger layers.'[8] Further, the order of such fossil groups is highly consistent throughout the world, even across different continents.

6. 'What Does the Fossil Record Show?' BioLogos, accessed July 2021, https://biologos.org/common-questions/what-does-the-fossil-record-show

7. National Academy of Sciences, 'Evidence Supporting Biological Evolution'.

8. 'What Does the Fossil Record Show?' BioLogos.

This fossil group replacement is known as the principle of faunal succession. The fossil evidence for evolution is persuasive simply because of the worldwide consistency of the sequence of fossils from the earliest to the more recent.[9] For example, strata with single-celled organisms are older than those that are multi-celled, invertebrate fossils are older than vertebrates. In no place has this sequence been overturned. Similarly, mammals are never found in the Devonian (the fish) strata, or human fossils with dinosaur fossils. The conclusion of all this is that descent with modification has occurred or, in other words, biological evolution.

Comparative anatomy, the comparison of structural similarities between organisms and in many ways similar to the much earlier studies of Carl Linneas, provides strong evidence for the family relationship of species and of common ancestry. Also, importantly, these family trees constructed by anatomical means show strikingly similar – but independent – verification of the family tree as do the molecular findings such as the proteins including cytochrome c, as explained above. That is, the closer the relationship, the greater the structural similarity. This is known as homology. One well-known example, but no less true for that, is the pentadactyl (five-digit) limb, found in most vertebrates (animals with a spine), which has a very similar bone structure and pattern. These forelimbs of whales, dogs, bats and humans, all mammals, are structurally very similar. Each has the same number of bones which are arranged in the same way. The main difference is that the size and shape of each bone has been modified over time to serve a slightly different purpose. There are many other examples of structural homology.

Some structures exist in organisms that have no apparent function at all but are present because of a past common ancestor. These vestigial, normally non-useful, structures are found in a wide

9. National Academy of Sciences, 'Evidence Supporting Biological Evolution'.

range of species, such as the leaves on some cacti, wings on flightless birds and hind leg bones in whales. In humans for example the tail bone or coccyx is a vestige of the mammalian tail.[10] Interestingly, there are over a hundred medical reports of babies born with tails, where the signal that stops the process of vertebrate elongation during development fails to function properly. It is estimated that in humans alone there are more than a hundred vestigial anomalies, some being anatomical, others being physiological, and still others behavioural.[11]

Embryology, the study of embryos, also provides good evidence for evolution. During early development, it is not really possible to visually tell the difference between a cat, a human, or a bat embryo, as they are so similar.[12] Structures that do not exist in adults may often appear in their embryonic forms. A good example is that of gill slits and tails, which are present in all vertebrate embryos, including humans, and which disappear in the adult forms of land species but remain in the adults of aquatic species such as fish and some amphibians.[13] The gene sequences active in these early embryonic stages are very similar to one another, whether it be fruit flies, worms, or humans, again suggesting an earlier common ancestor.

Biogeography is the study of the geographical distribution of biological organisms. Species that appear to be closely related also tend to be geographically close. Darwin was particularly interested in studying species on islands, and he found that they seemed to

10. Laura Spinney, 'Five Things Humans No Longer Need', *New Scientist*, 19 May 2008.

11. Kara Rogers, '7 Vestigial Features of the Human Body', *Encyclopedia Britannica*, accessed 15 November 2021, https://www.britannica.com/list/7-vestigial-features-of-the-human-body

12. Mary Dowd, 'How Does Embryology Provide Evidence for Evolution?' Sciencing.com, accessed 28 May 2022, https://sciencing.com/how-does-embryology-provide-evidence-for-evolution-13719067.html.

13. 'Similarities of Embryos', New England Complex Systems Institute, https://necsi.edu/similarities-of-embryos.

be most closely related to species found on the nearest mainland. In his study of the finches on the Galapagos Islands, an isolated group of volcanic islands off South America, he found a number of different finch species, with each species inhabiting a different island. These species were not only similar to one other, but they were also similar to a single species on the mainland. Darwin's conclusions, after much work, were that these Galapagos finches were descended from individual birds of this single species from the mainland which had somehow reached the islands in the distant past. Because the island habitats were different from the mainland, the selection pressures upon these finches also differed, resulting in new traits being favoured and the evolution of new finch species. Recent DNA analyses have confirmed these relationships and have proved that Darwin's original hypothesis on this was correct.[14]

More broadly, it is the movement of tectonic plates over long periods of time which determines the geographical distribution of different species.[15] Our planet was once joined together by a single giant super-continent called Pangea. Around 200 million years ago, Pangea gradually broke up, resulting in the separation of the southern half, Gondwanaland, which in turn gradually split into Antarctica, Africa, Australia, South America and India. It is fascinating that the broad species groups which evolved before the breakup of Pangea are now distributed worldwide, whereas those that evolved later have a narrower distribution range. For example, the marsupials of Australia, where the young are carried in a pouch such as kangaroos, koalas, and wombats, arose after this continent became separated and, due to its isolation, produced unique animals not found elsewhere. However, different marsupials can also be

14. Nicholas Wade, 'Finch DNA Shows Darwin Was Right', *The New York Times*, 11 May 1999.

15. J. Brendan Murphy and Tjeerd H. Andel, 'Plate Tectonics', *Encyclopedia Britannica*, accessed 15 November 2021, https://www.britannica.com/science/plate-tectonics

found in South America and are related, because it was previously attached to Australia as a single continent. An 'original' marsupial species would have lived on this continent which gradually evolved into different species upon continental separation, to better adapt to their new environments.

Genomics, Including Human Evolution

For this section, I am especially grateful to two Christian geneticists who have been at the cutting edge of our worldwide understanding of genomics in relation to human evolution, namely Francis Collins and Graeme Finlay. Francis Collins is the celebrated former head of the Human Genome Project, and I would like to flag up his excellent book which includes his Christian story.[16] Genomics is a very recent branch of biology, starting in a major way in 1990 with the launch of the Human Genome Project, and is a development of genetics. Every living organism has a genome, which is its complete set of DNA containing all of the information needed to develop and maintain the organism. I would also like to highlight the work of Dr Graeme Finlay, another expert in this field who is also a Christian. He explains that, from comparing the human genome with those of other primates, human evolution has now been conclusively proven.[17] The common ancestry of humans and other higher primates is now proven because we have randomly formed genetic markers uniquely shared by ourselves and by other primates. There are three types of biomarker in particular: first, our chromosome arrangement; second, certain identical 'pseudogenes'; and thirdly, identical packets of genetic information known as retrotransposons. These three genetic markers can only have arisen

16. Francis S. Collins, *The Language of God*. Simon and Schuster UK Ltd, London, 2007.

17. Graeme Finlay, 'Homo divinus: the Ape that Bears God's Image', *Science and Christian Belief*. Vol. 15, no. 1, 2003, pp.17–40.

once, in a common ancestor. That is, because of the very recent evidence that we share many unambiguous genetic markers with the great apes, our close biological relationship with them has now been established. Graeme Finlay presents a large body of information on the above, evidence that is both unequivocal and indisputable.

Biologically, humans are great apes or hominids, with our closest relatives being chimpanzees and bonobos.[18] DNA and fossil evidence shows that humans shared a common ancestor with chimpanzees and bonobos around six million years ago.

Modern humans (*Homo sapiens*, which is Latin for 'wise man') originated in Africa within the past 200,000 years and evolved from their most likely ancestor, *Homo erectus*, or 'upright man', an extinct human species that lived between 1.9 million and 135,000 years ago.[19] As humans migrated out of Africa some 50,000 to 80,000 years ago, they encountered two earlier, primitive, humans known as Neanderthal and Denisovan man. These humans are now extinct but from genomic analyses, it is clear that we co-existed and interbred with them. For example, the proportion of Neanderthal-derived DNA of those people living outside Africa is 1.5–2.1 percent. Nine of these genes are known to be associated with susceptibility to conditions such as type 2 diabetes, lupus and Crohn's disease, which signifies the wealth of information now at our disposal from the modern tool of genomics.

I will discuss in a later chapter some implications of biological evolution in the light of Scripture and particularly with the early chapters of Genesis. How do they equate? How do we need to

18. Ann Gibbons, 'Bonobos Join Chimps as Closest Human Relatives', *Science*, 13 June 2012.

K. Prufer, et al, 'The Bonobo Genome Compared with the Chimpanzee and Human Genome', *Nature*, 28 June 2012, 486 (7404), p 527–531.

19. 'Evolution of Modern Humans', Yourgenome.org. Accessed 21 July 2021, https://www.yourgenome.org/stories/evolution-of-modern-humans/

interpret Genesis, given the scientific light that we now have about evolution? But first, let us explore in some detail the age of the Earth and the universe, as these are also relatively recent scientific discoveries and may well have a bearing on our worldview.

Chapter Twenty-Five
The Age of the Earth and Universe

With the tools now available to us, the ages of the Earth and of the universe have now been calculated with great accuracy. Earth, by various independent techniques, has been found to be 4.5 billion years old whilst the universe, by astronomical means, has been found to be 13.8 billion years old.[1] The evidence for an old Earth is now conclusive and, as is the case with biological evolution, is not in question by those working in the field. The age of the Earth is relevant to biology, as an old Earth would be necessary for biological evolution to have occurred.

Before looking at the accurate radiometric dating evidence, let us spend a little time on the non-radiometric evidence for an old Earth and what this tells us. One group of these is the study of reliable 'annual clocks'. A prime example is the study of annual tree rings, with each ring being a single year of a tree's life; an increase in growth in the spring, followed by a slowing down in

1. R. M. Hazen, 'How Old is Earth, and How Do We Know?' *Evolution: Education and Outreach*, 3, 2010, pp.198–205.

P. Senter, 'The Age of the Earth and Its Importance to Biology', *The American Biology Teacher*. Vol. 75, issue 4, April 2013, pp.251–256.

'How are the Ages of the Earth and Universe Calculated?' BioLogos. Accessed 10 January 2020, https://biologos.org/common-questions/how-are-the-ages-of-the-earth-and-universe-calculated.

Nola Taylor Tillman, 'How Old is Earth?' *Space*, 20 August 2021.

'How Are the Ages of the Earth and Universe Calculated?' BioLogos.

Maria Temming, 'What Is the Age of the Universe?' *Sky and Telescope*. Last modified 18 July 2014, https://skyandtelescope.org/astronomy-resources/age-of-the-universe/

the winter. Although an individual tree can live to an absolute maximum of a few thousand years, overlapping periods are studied from variations in ring thickness which is wider in wetter years and narrower in drier years. By comparing the ring variations of living trees with those of dead ones such as buried logs, tree dating (or dendrochronology) has shown a continuous tree age of 26,000 years.[2] Another type of 'annual clock' study is from varves. These are the annual layers or deposits from sedimentary rocks, found in lakes and some other marine areas. One study, from glacial lakes in Sweden, has shown such deposits to go back 13,527 years with another from Japan which goes back 29,100 years.[3] A third type of 'annual clock' is from Polar ice cores, with annual layers which can clearly be identified. A study from Greenland has shown one area to be over 40,000 years old. Another, from Lake Vostok in Antarctica, has a recorded time span estimation of 420,000 years.[4] These annual clocks are instructive in that they show that the Earth is fairly old and is most certainly over 400,000 years old. The question of 'but how old, exactly' has now been definitively answered by radiometric testing, which we will now consider.

Radiometric dating, developed just over a century ago, makes use of radioactive isotopes. These are variations of a chemical element that have unstable nuclei and so emit excess energy by spontaneously emitting radiation in the form of alpha, beta, or gamma rays. All chemical elements have one or more radioactive isotopes. Although more than 1,800 radioactive isotopes of the various elements are known, some of these are found in nature, with the rest being

2. R. M. Hazen, 'How Old is Earth, and How Do We Know?' *Evolution: Education and Outreach.*

3. R. M. Hazen, 'How Old is Earth, and How Do We Know?' *Evolution: Education and Outreach.*

4. P. Senter, 'The Age of the Earth and Its Importance to Biology', *The American Biology Teacher.*

produced artificially as the direct products of nuclear reactions or indirectly as the radioactive descendants of these products. Each 'parent' radioactive isotope eventually decays into one or at most a few stable isotope 'daughters' specific to that parent.

The isotopes of the radioactive elements found in nature can be found in rocks, in water, and in the air. As they are unstable, they break down or decay. But, their rates of decay are very precise and predictable, just like the ticking of a clock. If you start with one million atoms of a particular isotope, half will decay over a period of time which is known as its 'half-life'. The best-known dating method uses carbon-14 which has a half-life of 5,730 years. As all living organisms ingest carbon, whether by physical food in animals or as carbon dioxide in plants; although 99 per cent is in the form of stable carbon-12, a very small proportion of carbon is in the form of the radioactive isotope, carbon-14. Once an organism dies, this carbon-14 decays to nitrogen-14 at a very precise rate. So by measuring the proportion of carbon-14 to nitrogen-14, the age of a bone, wood, piece of hair, or other carbon-based objects can be accurately determined. Carbon-14 dating is effective for objects up to 50,000 years old, but for objects older than this, isotopes with much longer half-lives are used. In geology, there are three main radioactive isotopes used as radiometric clocks, adopting a similar principle to that of carbon. These are potassium-40 with a half-life of 1.248 billion years, uranium-238 (of 4.468 billion years), and rubidium-87 (of 47 billion years).[5]

Uranium-238 dating is based upon the breakdown of uranium-238 to its daughter isotope, lead-206. This can be used to date the solidification of igneous rock which at one time would have been molten magma. As the magma cools and hardens, their radioactive

5. R. M. Hazen, 'How Old is Earth, and How Do We Know?' *Evolution: Education and Outreach.*

isotopes become locked into place and start to decay. By measuring the proportion of uranium-238 to lead-206 (known as U-Pb decay) in these samples in relation to the half-life of uranium-238, the age of these rocks can be accurately determined. The oldest rocks found on Earth are the Acasta Gneiss in northwestern Canada which are 4.03 billion years old, but rocks older than 3.5 billion years have been found on all continents.[6] Further, some small mineral grains known as zirconium silicate crystals found in Australia have been found to reach 4.4 billion years. This sets a lower age for the Earth, as the planet itself must be older than anything that lies on its surface, and older rocks probably existed and re-melted in tectonic events. Scientists have dated meteorites that comprise part of the asteroid belt and have found consistent ages of 4.55 billion years. Similarly, moon rocks, which would have solidified at the same time as the Earth's crust, give ages of 4.53 billion years.[7] Meteorite samples from Mars which have fallen to Earth have been dated to 4.5 billion years old.[8]

Experimental evidence confirms that rates of radioactive decay are not significantly affected by being subjected to environmental changes, whether these are extremes of heat, pressure, or strong magnetic fields. That is, rates of radioactive decay are constant. Further, radiometric ages agree with the ages found by other methods. For example, Uranium-thorium dating (U-Th) agrees with dendrochronological dates, and the radiocarbon dates from varves, tree rings, and polar ice cores are all in agreement and accord with their 'annual clocks'.

Different radiometric methods correspond with one another,

6. Nola Taylor Tillman, 'How Old is Earth?' *Space*.

7. P. Senter, 'The Age of the Earth and Its Importance to Biology', *The American Biology Teacher*.

8. Nola Taylor Tillman, 'How Old is Earth?' *Space*.

examples being for the age of the St Severin meteorite at 4.5 billion years, having been confirmed by three different techniques: Rubidium-strontium dating (Rb-Sr), Argon-argon dating (Ar-Ar) and Samarium-neodymium dating (Sm-Nd), and with the age of the Olivenza and Gurarena meteorites at 4.5 billion years by the Rb-Sr and Ar-Ar dating methods.[9]

The Age of the Universe

What about the ages of the stars, the galaxies, and the universe itself? Well, we could do a calculation by looking at the speed of light. Light travels extremely fast – 186,000 miles (300,000 kilometres) per second. Although on Earth the delay due to light travel time is a tiny fraction of a second, in space the distances are so vast that the light takes a significant amount of time to travel to us: 8.3 minutes from the sun, 4.3 years from the nearest star and about 8,500 years from the centre of the Milky Way galaxy. This delay means that we don't see these objects as they are right now, but as they were when the light left. The universe actually works as a sort of 'time machine', in which we can see into the past simply by looking far away. The Andromeda galaxy, a relatively 'near neighbour' to our own Milky Way galaxy, is 2.3 million light-years away. That is, we are seeing it as it was 2.3 million years ago. In recent decades, astronomers have found galaxies that are several billion light-years away. So, as this light has been taking billions of years to reach us, then the universe must be at least that old. This is a completely independent calculation from, for example, radiometric dating of the Earth or of the solar system, but both methods point to the same conclusion: that the universe is billions of years old.[10]

9. P. Senter, 'The Age of the Earth and Its Importance to Biology', *The American Biology Teacher*.

10. 'How Are the Ages of the Earth and Universe Calculated?' BioLogos.

An entirely different method from the above, via astronomical means, has now determined the age of the universe to be precisely 13.79 +/- 0.02 billion years. We know that most other galaxies are moving away from our own at speeds which are proportional to their distances. We know the expansion rate of the universe, so we can 'rewind' to the point where everything was contained at one point and calculate the length of time from that moment (the Big Bang) to the present. It is a little more complicated than that, as we need to know the history of the expansion rate. If we assume that the expansion rate is constant over time, the age of the universe as a whole is about ten billion years. However, astronomers have recently determined how the expansion rate changes with time. We now know that early on the expansion rate of the universe was slowing down, but now it is speeding up. Using careful measurements of this change in expansion rate, the age of the universe has recently been accurately determined.[11]

11. 'How Are the Ages of the Earth and Universe Calculated?' BioLogos. Maria Temming, 'What Is the Age of the Universe?' *Sky and Telescope*.

Chapter Twenty-Six
Biological Evolution Compared with Evolutionism and Other Views

Let us reflect a little on different viewpoints amongst Christians and others concerning 'origins'. First, there is the world of difference between evolutionism and biological evolution. Evolutionism is an atheistic worldview that holds that all of reality can be explained by science. That is, God is not included in this paradigm. However, biological evolution is different: it is that science is limited to explaining the natural world, and that the supernatural, including God and miracles, is also included within this reality. A Christian approach can fully accept the Bible as the inspired and authoritative word of God whilst at the same time accepting that the science of biological evolution is the best way of understanding how God brought about the diversity of life on Earth. This represents my own view: that biological evolution, as seen in a Christian context, is simply God's mechanism for bringing about and continuing his created order, both at the beginning and throughout history.

This has been termed 'evolutionary creationism' or EC.[1] But, what do other people think? One survey undertaken in 2019 of the general US population showed that virtually all scientists, a significant proportion of them being Christians, accepted that

1. 'How is Evolutionary Creation Different From Evolutionism, Intelligent Design and Creationism?' BioLogos. Accessed 8 October 2020, https://biologos.org/common-questions/how-is-biologos-different-from-evolutionism-intelligent-design-and-creationism

humans have evolved over time.[2] Most of the US population (81% of all US adults) also shared this view. On the other hand, almost four in ten white Evangelical Protestants rejected biological evolution. Further, 59 per cent of the US adult population believed that science and religion are in conflict, a figure which rose to 73 per cent of those who didn't regularly attend church services, and which was 50 per cent amongst those who attended church frequently. This anti-evolution standpoint has not always been the case amongst the Christian community and is a relatively recent phenomenon. For example, the British historian James Moore wrote that 'with few exceptions, the leading Christian thinkers in Great Britain and America came to terms quite readily with Darwinism and evolution' and the US sociologist George Marsden reported that 'with the exception of Harvard's Louis Agassiz, virtually every American Protestant zoologist and botanist accepted some form of evolution by the early 1870s.'[3]

All Christians accept that God is our creator. That is, we are all 'creationists' and these beliefs accord entirely, for example, with the Nicene Creed, which begins 'I believe in one God, the Father Almighty, maker of heaven and Earth, and of all things visible and invisible.' I wish to recommend the admirable book *Reclaiming Genesis* by Melvin Tinker, which provides an impressive understanding of Genesis and its meaning for our contemporary world, and with emphasis on the Biblical texts and their interpretation.[4]

2. David Masci, 'For Darwin Day, 6 Facts About the Evolution Debate', Pew Research Centre. Last modified 11 February 2019, https://www.pewresearch.org/fact-tank/2019/02/11/darwin-day/

3. Denis R. Alexander, 'Can a Christian Believe in Evolution?' Evangelical Alliance. Last modified 1 May 2005, https://www.eauk.org/church/resources/theological-articles/can-a-christian-believe-in-evolution.cfm.

4. Melvin Tinker, *Reclaiming Genesis*. Monarch Books, UK, 20 August 2010.

There are other creationist viewpoints held by Christians besides that of evolutionary creationism (EC), which is my own view. Another one is known as young earth creationism (YEC), the belief that a faithful reading of Scripture commits Christians to accept that the Earth is young, between 6,000 and 10,000 years old, that God created the universe in six literal twenty-four-hour days, that Scripture is not compatible with the idea that humans share a common ancestry with other living things on Earth, and that evolution is a direct threat to Christianity. Another viewpoint is what is known as old earth creationism (OEC), the belief that there is good scientific evidence for the great age of the Earth (4.5 billion years) and the universe (13.8 billion years). The prevailing view of OEC is that each of the six days of creation in Genesis chapter one refers to long periods of time. OEC does not accept the common ancestry of all life forms but endorses a theory of progressive creation in which God miraculously created new species at key moments in the history of life. A fourth view is named intelligent design or ID. This viewpoint seeks to show that living organisms were created, but already in their current forms, by an intelligent designer. It rejects the theory of biological evolution but maintains that the development of life is a testable scientific hypothesis. The YEC, OEC and ID views that reject biological evolution have now been proved to be incorrect and continue an unnecessary conflict between science and Christianity, thus becoming a stumbling block to those considering Christianity.[5] Sadly, many people coming across such views, particularly well-educated younger people, may feel that they have to choose between Christianity and science, which is most certainly not correct. I wish to add that I am fortunate to have been educated in the sciences from a young age and have never considered these to be in conflict with the Christian faith.

5. 'How is Evolutionary Creation Different From Evolutionism, Intelligent Design and Creationism?' BioLogos.

I agree with the viewpoint expressed by the BioLogos Foundation, a Christian advocacy group established in 2007 by Dr Francis Collins of Human Genome Project renown, which seeks to reconcile evolution with the idea of God in this matter, namely that our intelligent God, our real 'intelligent designer', designed the universe with all its grandeur, beauty, and complexity, but that we have now uncovered through scientific discovery, and will continue to uncover, how God has done this. That is, 'scientific explanations complement a robust theological understanding of God's role as designer, creator and sustainer of the universe.'[6]

Before exploring a little in the next chapter how our scientific understanding of the world's beginning can equate with the book of Genesis, it should again be stressed that the greatest scientific authorities in the world accept biological evolution as factual. For example, the Royal Society of London, one of the world's most august scientific institutions, issued a statement on 11 April 2006 which described evolution as 'the best explanation for the development of life on Earth from its beginnings and for the diversity of species' and as 'rightly taught as an essential part of biology and science courses in schools, colleges and universities across the world.'[7] Their statement also emphasizes the importance of evolution in understanding and solving problems of practical importance in medicine and agriculture. Also, the Geological Society of London, which is the oldest national learned society in the world for the Earth sciences, and embodies the collective knowledge of nearly 10,000 Earth scientists worldwide, issued a statement, approved by their council and published on 11 April 2008 entitled 'Young

6. 'How is Evolutionary Creation Different From Evolutionism, Intelligent Design and Creationism?' BioLogos.

7. 'Royal Society Issues Statement on Evolution', NCSE (National Center for Science Education). Last modified 13 April 2006, https://ncse.ngo/royal-society-issues-statement-evolution

Earth Creationism, Creation Science and Intelligent Design', which included the following facts as 'being long-established beyond doubt':

> Planet Earth, along with the other planets in the solar system, was formed approximately 4,560 million years ago.
>
> Life has existed on Earth for thousands of millions of years. It has evolved into its current form by a combination of genetic variation and natural selection – and is likely to go on doing so for as long as it continues to exist.
>
> A close study of the structure and organisation of living animals and plants clearly indicates their common ancestry, and the succession of forms through the fossil record, as well as the genetic record contained in every living organism, provides powerful evidence of the reality of evolution.[8]

The above statements are unequivocal and accord with the understanding of human origins by almost all scientists worldwide, including the many scientists who hold Christian beliefs.

8. 'Young Earth Creationism, Creation Science and Intelligent Design.' A Statement by the Geological Society of London. Approved by Council 10 April, and published 11 April 2008.

Chapter Twenty-Seven
The Book of Genesis and Scientific Discovery

We have discussed the Big Bang, showing that the universe had a beginning, both in terms of space and time. We have also discussed 'fine-tuning', which shows that the universe and life itself only exist because of the fine precision of key physical laws. Both of these immense discoveries have only been made within the last fifty years and in my mind are in entire accord with the Christian teaching as found in the first verse of Genesis, chapter one: 'In the beginning God created the heavens and the Earth'. It is for the reader to decide, in the light of these findings: do these facts support the belief that it is God who created the world, as clearly stated in Scripture, or do these facts support atheistic unbelief? Which is the most likely?

In considering Genesis, it is important that Christian people should start with the premise that Scripture itself is a supernatural book. That is, it has been given to human beings as God's revelation to mankind. St Paul makes the following clear statement 'All Scripture is God-breathed and is useful for teaching, rebuking, correcting, and training in righteousness, so that the servant of God may be thoroughly equipped for every good work.' (2 Timothy 3:16–17.) In New Testament times the Scriptures being referred to were solely the Hebrew Scriptures, our Old Testament. These writers made it clear, as Jesus did, that these Scriptures were divine in nature and came from God himself.

Jesus, and the Jewish people of his day, regarded these accounts of their history and of God's dealings with them over many centuries as being deeply holy matters, full of divine truth, and of the greatest possible importance. We have already seen the extraordinary supernatural and prophetic nature of a large body of these ancient Scriptures and their fulfilment in Jesus as the Messiah in part three of this book. In my opinion, we need to understand the prime importance of Scripture as the divine revelation of God himself before we even begin to study and try to interpret the written accounts of creation in early Genesis and their teaching to us, with our modern, scientific, and twenty-first-century perspective.

One way of seeking to interpret what the divine nature of early Genesis is about is to consider the views concerning these sacred texts about the creation of the world in Genesis 1–2 in the centuries before our modern scientific era. That is, the views held by the Christian theologians before it was discovered that this universe and the world are very old and before our recent evolutionary understanding. It is assumed by many today that Darwin's theory of evolution was a watershed that shook the foundations of the Christian faith, not least because of the sharp contrast between biological evolution and the idea of a six-day creation. However, this literal six-day interpretation of Genesis 1–2 was by no means the only interpretation by the earlier theologians prior to geology and Darwin. For instance, Origen, a third-century theologian from Alexandria in Egypt, has given us a good example of early Christian thinking on creation. In Origen's two works, *On First Principles* and *Against Celsius*, where he wrote about the main doctrines of Christianity and defended them against pagan views, he wrote opposing the idea of a literal and historic interpretation of the six days of creation, presenting instead a symbolic interpretation.[1]

1. 'How Was the Genesis Account of Creation Interpreted Before Darwin?' BioLogos. Accesed 18 January 2019, https://biologos.org/common-questions/how-was-the-genesis-account-of-creation-interpreted-before-darwin

Similarly, St Augustine of Hippo, a theologian, philosopher, and North African bishop who lived between 354 and 430 AD and who is widely regarded as the most significant Christian thinker after St Paul, spent many years studying these early Genesis texts. In *The Literal Meaning of Genesis*, one of his great works, he argues that the first two chapters of Genesis were written to accommodate the understanding of the people at that time, for those living in a pre-scientific age. St Augustine maintained that the six-day creation story was told in a simpler, allegorical way. St Thomas Aquinas, the Italian theologian living between 1225 and 1274, was also especially interested in the relationship between science and Christianity and held a similar view to that of St Augustine, not least suggesting a single day for the act of creation.

Later, John Wesley, living in the eighteenth century and before Darwin, viewed the six-day creation story as being written in a manner appropriate to the original audience. Wesley wrote:

> The inspired penman in this history [Genesis] . . . [wrote] for the Jews first and, calculating his narratives for the infant state of the church, describes things by their outward sensible appearances, and leaves us, by further discoveries of the divine light, to be led into the understanding of the mysteries couched under them.

In a similar vein, in the USA in the nineteenth century, perhaps the greatest conservative theologian of the time, B. B. Warfield of Princeton Theological Seminary, accepted evolution as providing the correct scientific account of human origins. He believed that hearing God's voice in Scripture and the findings of solid scientific work were compatible with one another.

I am grateful to the writer who has researched and written the above about the thinking of these highly respected earlier Christian theologians.[2] He concludes that the history of Christian thought has not been consistently dominated by proponents of a literal interpretation of the early Genesis creation story. The discoveries of modern science should neither be seen as the instigator of some abandonment of trust in Scripture, nor as contradictory to Scripture, but as guideposts towards a proper understanding of Scripture's meaning.

It is important to see the context (known as hermeneutics within theology) in which Genesis was written: not as a scientific textbook for modern twenty-first-century humans, but for a people that God had chosen for himself. Genesis was first written for the ancient Hebrews, a pre-scientific people. God was describing his creation in terms of near-Eastern cosmology rather than in modern, scientific terms. This is an example of 'accommodation' in Scripture.[3] John Calvin, the Protestant reformer who lived from 1509 to 1564, wrote that the Bible is not an astronomical, geographical, or biological textbook, but that in interpreting the Bible we need to realise that God 'adjusts' his revelation to the capacities of the human mind and heart. So, revelation needed to be scaled down or 'accommodated' for us in order to speak to our limited abilities.[4] This is likely to have been what happened with the six-day creation story.

The first chapter of Genesis describes the world as the ancient Hebrews saw it. Thus we see that the world contains a 'vault' to separate the waters above from the waters below, and with the

2. 'How Was the Genesis Account of Creation Interpreted Before Darwin?' BioLogos. Accessed 18 January 2019, https://biologos.org/common-questions/how-was-the-genesis-account-of-creation-interpreted-before-darwin

3. Alister E. McGrath, *Science and Religion: A New Introduction*. Wiley-Blackwell, 2nd edition, 12 January 2010.

4. McGrath, *Science and Religion*.

Tom Ingebritsen, 'Does Genesis 1 Teach Modern Science?' InterVarsity Emerging Scholars Network. Last modified 15 January 2014, https://blog.emergingscholars.org/2014/01/does-genesis-1-teach-modern-science/

moon and the stars being placed within this vault in order to give light and serve as signs. Obviously, we describe the world very differently in our modern age, but what we see is that God humbled himself in order to accommodate their understanding, just as he later humbled himself in his incarnation. That is, then as now, God provides eternal truths in ways that we are able to understand.[5]

Once we have understood this ancient context, the early text provides some very interesting information for us. For example, the spaces created in the first three days of the six-day creation are then inhabited in the following three days. So, God creates light and darkness on the first day, and the sun, moon, and stars on the fourth day in order to occupy the light and dark. Similarly, on the second day, we are given the waters above and beneath the Earth, which are then occupied by the birds of the sky and the sea creatures on the fifth day. Then, in the same pattern, on the third day, God created dry land, which is then occupied by land animals, including us, on the sixth day. This literary structure suggests that what we have been given is a powerful poetic account of the creation story, not a chronological one.[6] In Genesis chapter one, we are also given an account of God's supremacy over the 'gods' of Israel's neighbours. Genesis 1:16 says, 'God made two great lights – the greater light to govern the day and the lesser light to govern the night. He also made the stars.' What this statement does is speak powerfully to the ancient Hebrews that God himself is the only one to be worshipped, and with the pagan gods affiliated with the sun, moon, and stars as worshipped by

5. Michael Lehmann, 'Theology Before Darwin: Defusing the Dilemma', BioLogos. Last modified 4 September 2019, https://biologos.org/articles/theology-before-darwin-defusing-the-dilemma.

6. Lehmann, 'Theology Before Darwin: Defusing the Dilemma', BioLogos.

their neighbours being stripped of any kind of divinity, as God himself had created the sun, moon and stars himself.[7]

The Bible provides us with great wisdom about God, but it is a mistake to treat it as a scientific textbook. The ancient Hebrews would have understood, for example, the relationship between the six days of creation as expressed in early Genesis and with God's denunciation of polytheism as in Genesis 1:16. The church fathers, the early theologians, would have understood the meaning of the creation account: that it was God alone who created the world, that he created it out of nothing, and that Jesus Christ is the key to everything, including our own salvation.[8]

There were, in fact, two creation accounts in early Genesis: the first in Genesis 1:1–2, juxtaposed to a second creation account beginning in Genesis 2:4. In the first account, we see God calling the cosmos – that is heaven and Earth, and all that is in them – into existence. Then in the rest of Genesis, starting in Genesis chapter two, we have the account of what developed from God's initial creation and how humans responded to God's call to be his image in the world. What we see is a wonderful literary depth to these early creation accounts that provide us with a full theological picture of God's work in creation and where the chronology of creation is not the main focus.[9]

The creation accounts in Genesis were given in order to provide a major contrast with the various other creation stories from the surrounding pagan cultures when Genesis was written.[10] The Hebrew account in early Genesis was monotheistic, teaching that there is only one God who is the creator of all, which was entirely different

7. Lehmann, 'Theology Before Darwin: Defusing the Dilemma', BioLogos.

8. Lehmann, 'Theology Before Darwin: Defusing the Dilemma', BioLogos.

9. 'How Long are the Days of Genesis 1?' BioLogos. Accessed 16 June 2021, https://biologos.org/common-questions/how-long-are-the-days-of-genesis-1.

10. William R. Harper, 'The Origin of Man and His First State of Innocence: Genesis II', *The Biblical World*. University of Chicago Press, vol. 3, no. 2, February 1894, pp. 97–108.

from the creation stories in the surrounding pagan nations before or during that time. For example, the Babylonian and Egyptian creation stories were polytheistic; the Hebrew account teaches that one God created with wisdom and order, not out of the chaos of war between the gods, as in the pagan creation stories; further, it teaches that creation occurred at God's command, not from a power struggle between the gods. Finally, it teaches that human beings are the pinnacle of God's creation and are made in his image (known as *imago Dei*), in contrast to the pagan creation stories where mankind was created only as a minor player and as an afterthought.[11]

For modern readers, as for the original audience, we can see the profound truths contained within Genesis chapter one. In a beautifully crafted and short text we are taught, first, about God's sovereignty; second, the goodness of creation; and third, the honoured place of humankind as the bearers of God's image. The physical world is spoken of in simple terms, based upon how it appears, so that all people may understand it. The common language of the text has enabled it to be accessible to people of all times and cultures, thus helping the communication of the gospel throughout the world. We have received the same essential truths of Genesis chapter one over many centuries; namely that there is one sovereign God who has made light from darkness, has created an ordered world out of chaos, and who has filled an empty world with good creatures. We need not fear the prospect of unreliable and impulsive non-existent gods, but are now able to trust in the one true God who made us in his image and who has declared us to be 'very good'.[12]

A key purpose of God, as described in the Biblical Genesis Hebrew

11. Tom Ingebritsen, 'The Message of Genesis 1', InterVarsity Emerging Scholars Network. Last modified 9 January 2014, https://blog.emergingscholars.org/2014/01/message-genesis-1/

12. D. Haarsma and L. Haarsma, 'Comparing Interpretations of Genesis 1', BioLogos. Last modified 9 January 2008, https://biologos.org/articles/comparing-interpretations-of-genesis-1

account in the sixth century BC, was to create an exclusive people for himself who would worship him alone, rather than turn to the pagan, untrue gods in these other cultures. This is later brought out in the commandments (Exodus 20:3–4): 'You shall have no other gods before me. You shall not make for yourself an image in the form of anything in heaven above or on the earth beneath or in the waters below.'

Are we to conclude that the Genesis creation account is a myth, in the sense of being untrue, similar to the various pagan myths of the Near Eastern world? My belief is that the Hebrew account relates to actual historic events, but in a profound and poetic way. Kenneth Kitchen, a prominent Egyptologist and Christian, has stated:

> The ancient Near East did not historicize myth (i.e. read it as imaginary 'history'). In fact, exactly the reverse is true – there was, rather, a trend to 'mythologize' history, to celebrate actual historical events and people in mythological terms.[13]

So, in Genesis 1 we have, firstly, the cosmological background to the start of God's special relationship with mankind, then the human story, beginning with Adam and Eve and continuing throughout the human family as written in the remainder of Genesis, the rest of the Torah (the first five books of the Bible), the remainder of the Old Testament, the whole of the New Testament and beyond, up to and including our present day.[14] This was meant to be understood in a theological, revelatory, relational, and historical way, rather than in a scientific and empirical way.

13. K. A. Kitchen, *On the Reliability of the Old Testament*. William B. Eerdmans Publishing Co., annotated edition, 25 July 2006.

14. 'Understanding the Creation Story from Genesis', Zondervan Academic, last modified 1 May 2018, https://zondervanacademic.com/blog/understanding-the-creation-story-from-genesis

What we read is that God created two human beings as his first special creation and for his first special relationship: namely, Adam and Eve. These were truly special people because they were the first humans to be chosen to enjoy a close, intimate, relationship with God, which God always intended for them and for their descendants, in fact for the whole human race. As we are aware, they were warned by God (Genesis 2:17) not to eat from the tree of the knowledge of good and evil, for 'when you eat from it you will certainly die.' God, as with each of us, gave them free will. Unfortunately, they disobeyed God and thus began their spiritual separation and what is known as the 'fall'. This was catastrophic, both for them and for their descendants, where this separation was passed on. Thus began what is termed 'original sin'. It was so catastrophic for the human race that God himself had to come down as an incarnate human being in Jesus Christ in order to redeem and bring us back to him, by suffering and dying to atone for our sins in order to restore this broken relationship. The degree of Adam's and of our inherited sin in the sight of God can only really be understood by looking at the cost to God in providing the remedy. It was an extraordinary act of love and mercy. If we ever doubted our own sin, then let us look at the cross and the price that God needed to pay in order to provide the reconciliation.

Further light on our relationship with Adam and with Jesus Christ is given in the New Testament. For example:

> But Christ has indeed been raised from the dead, the firstfruits of those who have fallen asleep. For since death came through a man, the resurrection of the dead comes also through a man. For as in Adam all die, so in Christ all will be made alive.
>
> (1 Corinthians 15:20–22)

Also, in Romans 5:12–21:

> Therefore, just as sin entered the world through one man, and death through sin, and in this way death came to all people, because all sinned.
>
> (Romans 5:12)

> But the gift is not like the trespass. For if the many died by the trespass of the one man, how much more did God's grace and the gift that came by the grace of the one man, Jesus Christ, overflow to the many!
>
> (Romans 5:15)

> For just as through the disobedience of the one man the many were made sinners, so also through the obedience of the one man the many will be made righteous.
>
> (Romans 5:19)

> So that, just as sin reigned in death, so also grace might reign through righteousness to bring eternal life through Jesus Christ our Lord.
>
> (Romans 5:21)

It is clear to me that the above passages of Scripture are referring to a real, historic couple and to real events. Early Genesis was not a work of fiction. This is supported by references to Adam in genealogies in Scripture. These can be found in three places: 1 Chronicles chapter one; Luke chapter three; and in Jude. Although these are not direct lists of father-son relationships, they are surely there to show that Adam and Eve were a real, historic couple. Also, Jesus himself quoted Genesis 1:27 and 2:24 when he was talking about marriage and divorce in Matthew 19:4–6.[15]

15. Kathryn Applegate, 'Why I Think Adam Was a Real Person in History', BioLogos. Last modified 11 June 2018.

The Genesis creation text itself seems to imply that there were other humans present around the time of Adam and Eve. We have that old chestnut of who was Cain's wife, the wife of their eldest son? It could not have been his sister, as incest was banned under Hebrew law. There would also have been problems with inbreeding, with recessive genes coming to the fore, analogous to that of haemophilia or porphyria, as in Queen Victoria's family. When Cain killed his brother Abel and had to wander, he was very afraid: 'whoever finds me will kill me' (Genesis 4:14). Who was he afraid of? It certainly suggests people outside of his family. When Cain builds a city (Genesis 4:17), the implication is that there were large numbers of people already living.[16]

Where does our scientific understanding meet with Adam and Eve, in the light of our recent understanding of biological evolution? There are several possibilities. In fact, Gerald Rau has proposed six possible ways of reconciling science with the Genesis account, which range from a completely literal understanding, right through to the total absence of God.[17] His own view is based upon the idea of *Homo divinus*, where the six days of creation are not a scientific description of our origins, and where Adam and Eve were Neolithic representatives of all mankind whom God called into a special relationship with himself. We are special because God chose to inter-relate with us, and because we were given the responsibility to care for the Earth.[18] This view is shared by many, including myself.

I am grateful to Professor R. J. Berry, an evangelical Christian and emeritus professor of genetics at London University, for my

16. Applegate, 'Why I Think Adam Was a Real Person in History', BioLogos.

17. Gerald Rau, Mapping the Origins Debate: Six Models of the Beginning of Everything, IVP Academic, 31 January 2013.

18. Ruth M. Bancewics, 'Homo divinus', *Science and Belief*, July 2015.

greater understanding. I include the following points based upon what he has written: There is overwhelming, compelling evidence (particularly in view of our genetic discoveries in the past thirty years) that, biologically, we share a common ancestry with other animals.[19] This cannot be ignored. Maybe we are still in a similar position to that of Galileo, where much of the church had to revise its thinking and accept the heliocentric nature of the Earth, in view of what he discovered. This did not affect our view of the authority of Scripture at that time, and neither should it now.

Professor Berry has written that the Earth's history, stretching over millions of years, was widely accepted long before Darwin proposed the theory of evolution. The Earth's long history is therefore independent of what he discovered and should not be controversial. Further, primates only appeared fairly recently in evolutionary history, with the earliest human fossils (*Homo sapiens*) appearing around 200,000 years ago. All the scientific evidence points to the human population not having dipped below a few thousand within the last 200,000 years. Professor Berry quotes the Revd Dr John Stott, who suggested that the biological species *Homo sapiens* was later transformed into *Homo divinus* without any physical change, and it was at this point that Adam was the first to be made in God's image (*imago Dei*), as written in Genesis 1:27. That is, the first creature to be made with the capacity to respond and relate to God. In other words, the first spiritual human being. This, to me, seems to be the beginning of God's revelation to us, a more recent spiritual event but separate from the biological event, which would have happened much earlier in history. The Genesis account describes Adam as a Neolithic farmer. This first spiritual creation, which involved an initial perfect relationship with God,

19. R. J. Berry, 'A Response to Dermot O'Callaghan,' *Science & Christian Belief*. Vol. 23, no. 1, April 2011, pp.69–72.

but also the gift of free will, was at some stage marred due to Adam's sin, leading to spiritual death and original sin for all who came after Adam. The only way to restore this was by the coming of God himself in the person of Jesus Christ to be our atoning, substitutionary, sacrifice. Christians recognise this, not just by what the Scriptures teach, but also from personal experience; the practical problem of indwelling human sin on the one hand, and by our acceptance of the sacrifice of Jesus Christ, which leads to a personal, restored relationship with God and to a life-changing experience of the indwelling Holy Spirit, on the other.

The above, to me, represents the best way of reconciling what Scripture is teaching us and with biological evolution, the latter of which cannot be ignored or argued against without flying in the face of concrete evidence, particularly in view of the genetic evidence of the past thirty years.

The above view is one of several amongst evolutionary creationists, of which I am one. The following is an excellent summing up in the final chapter of a book written by a group of eminent theologians and scientists, edited by R. J Berry and T. A. Noble.[20]

> Whither have the contributors to this book brought us? We believe they have established three critical principles:
>
> First, an insistence that as new information emerges, Scripture, whilst God-given and authoritative, must be re-examined and may require reinterpreting. Christians of a former age had no doubts that the sun moves around the Earth and supported their ideas from the Bible (e.g. Psalms 19:4–6; 96:10); nowadays we unhesitatingly interpret the passages which seemed to speak of a fixed Earth in other ways.

20. R. J. Berry and T. A. Noble, 'Epilogue: The Sea of Faith: Darwin Didn't Drain It', *Darwin, Creation and the Fall: Theological Challenges*. Inter-Varsity Press (IVP), UK, 19 June 2009.

> Second, an awareness of the compelling genetic and fossil evidence that human beings have descended from an ape-like line, and that we are therefore related to other living beings.
>
> Third, the uniqueness of human beings as the only creatures made in God's image, albeit 'fallen' so that life in fellowship with God is now only possible because of Christ's redeeming and reconciling death.

It is the conviction of these writers that there is no conflict between Holy Scripture and modern science. The idea that Christian faith and science are in conflict is a myth propagated by humanists for ideological reasons, but sadly they are helped by sincere Christian believers who think they are defending Holy Scripture when in fact they are doing no more than defending interpretations of Holy Scripture which are sadly inadequate.

Bibliography

Arapović, Borislav. *Bibelns sidenväg*, 1998.

Armstrong, Aaron. 'Does God Make Himself Known?' The Gospel Project. https://gospelproject.lifeway.com/does-god-make-himself-known/

Bancewics, Ruth M. 'Homo divinus', *Science and Belief*, July 2015.

Beibl Byw – Wales to the World. The Union of Welsh Independents, 4 February 2016.

Begin Your Journey to Peace. Peace with God, Billy Graham Evangelistic Association UK, 2021.

Benner, Jeff A. *The Great Isaiah Scroll and the Masoretic Text*. Ancient Hebrew Research Center.

Berry, R. J. 'A Response to Dermot O'Callaghan,' *Science & Christian Belief*. Vol. 23, no. 1, April 2011.

Berry, R. J., and T. A. Noble, 'Epilogue: The Sea of Faith: Darwin Didn't Drain It', *Darwin, Creation and the Fall: Theological Challenges*. Inter-Varsity Press (IVP), UK, 19 June 2009.

Brown, Larry V. *A History of Christianity in Wales*. 11 May 2008, p.6.

Burrows, Millar. *The Dead Sea Scrolls*. Viking Press, New York, 1955, p.304. Quoted in Norman Geisler and William Nix, General Introduction to the Bible. Moody Press, Chicago, 1986.

Collins, Francis S. *The Language of God*. Simon and Schuster UK Ltd, London, 2007.

Connor, James A. *Pascal's Wager: The Man Who Played Dice with God*. Lion Books, 2007.

Eden, Caroline. 'On Board the Trans-Siberian Railway for a Centenary Ride,' *The Guardian*, 12 November 2016.

Ellis, George. 'Cosmology: The Untestable Multiverse', *Nature*. Vol. 469, 2011.

Finlay, Graeme. 'Homo divinus: the Ape that Bears God's Image', *Science and Christian Belief*. Vol. 15, no. 1, 2003.

Fruchtenbaum, Arnold. 'The Messianic Time Table According to Daniel the Prophet', *Jews for Jesus*, 20 April 2018.

Gibbons, Ann. 'Bonobos Join Chimps as Closest Human Relatives', *Science*, 13 June 2012.

Harper, William R. 'The Origin of Man and His First State of Innocence: Genesis II', *The Biblical World*. University of Chicago Press, vol. 3, no. 2, February 1894.

Hawking S., and L. Mlodinow, *The Grand Design*. Bantam Press, 2010.

Hazen, R. M. 'How Old is Earth, and How Do We Know?' Evolution: Education and Outreach, 3, 2010.

Johnstone, Patrick, Jason Mandryk, and Robyn Johnstone. *Operation World: 21st Century Edition*. Authentic Lifestyle, 2001.

Kitchen, K. A. *On the Reliability of the Old Testament*. William B. Eerdmans Publishing Co., annotated edition, 25 July 2006.

Konig, George and Ray. *100 Prophecies: Ancient Biblical Prophecies that Foretold the Future*. CreateSpace Independent Publishing Platform, October 2008.

Lewis, C. S. T*he Screwtape Letters: Letters from a Senior to a Junior Devil*. Collins, 2002, reprint edition.

Lewis, Revd. W. G. R. (Bill). Personal communication.

Lloyd-Jones, Martyn. *Romans: An Exposition of Chapters 3:20–4:25: Atonement and Justification*. The Banner of Truth Trust, 1970.

Manastireanu, Danut. 'Western Assistance in Theological Training for Romanian Evangelicals to 1989', East–West Church Ministry Report. Vol. 14, no. 3, summer 2006.

McGrath, Alister E. *Science and Religion: A New Introduction*. Wiley-Blackwell, 2nd edition, 12 January 2010.

National Academy of Sciences, 'Evidence Supporting Biological Evolution', in *Science and Creationism: A View from the National Academy of Sciences*. National Academies Press, 2nd revised edition, 1999.

Nolland, John. *The Gospel of Matthew: A Commentary on the Greek Text*. W. B. Eerdmans Publishing Co, 2005.

Paterlini, Marta. 'There Shall Be Order: The Legacy of Linnaeus in the Age of Molecular Biology', EMBO Reports (2007) 8, Oxford.

Poole, Michael. *God and the Big Bang – and Other Arguments About Science and Faith*. Christian Publicity Organisation, West Sussex, UK.

Prager, Dennis, and Alfred Kolatch, 'Did Jesus Fulfil Messianic Prophecy?' in *Jews for Jesus*. San Francisco, California, 94102, USA.

Prince, Derek. *Spiritual Warfare for the End Times: How to Defeat the Enemy*. Chosen Books, 2017.

Prince, Derek. *Spiritual Warfare*. Whitaker House, USA, 2001.

Prufer, K. et al, 'The Bonobo Genome Compared with the Chimpanzee and Human Genome', *Nature*, 28 June 2012, 486 (7404).

Ragnar, 'A Funny Gaffe – Fit for a Good Friday. The Puzzle of Psalm 22' in *Consider the Gospel*, April 2015.

Rau, Gerald. *Mapping the Origins Debate: Six Models of the Beginning of Everything*, IVP Academic, 31 January 2013.

Richards, Jay W. *List of Fine-Tuning Parameters*. Center for Science and Culture, Discovery Institute, 2020.

Rydelnik, Michael A. 'The Old Testament in the New Testament' in *The Moody Handbook of Messianic Prophecy, Studies and Expositions of the Messiah in the Old*

Testament, general editors M. Rydelnik and E. Blum. Moody Publishers, Chicago, 2019.

Ryle, J. C. Holiness: *Its Nature, Hindrances, Difficulties, and Roots*. The Banner of Truth Trust, 2015.

Senter, P. 'The Age of the Earth and Its Importance to Biology', *The American Biology Teacher*. Vol. 75, issue 4, April 2013.

Shalev, Baruch A. *100 Years of Nobel Prizes*. Americas Group Publications, 2002.

Slattery, Patrick. 'The Legacy of the Welsh Revival 1904–1905', *Headline*, summer 2004, Methodist Evangelicals Together (MET).

Spinney, Laura. 'Five Things Humans No Longer Need', *New Scientist*, 19 May 2008.

Stead, William T., G. Campbell Morgan, and Arthur Goodrich, and Evan Roberts. *The Welsh Revival & the Story of the Welsh Revival: As Told by Eyewitnesses Together With a Sketch of Evan Roberts and His Message to the World*. Trumpet Press, August 2015.

Steer, Roger. *George Müller: Delighted in God*. Christian Focus, 20 March 2015.

Tillman, Nola Taylor. 'How Old is Earth?' *Space*, 20 August 2021.

Tinker, Melvin. *Reclaiming Genesis*. Monarch Books, UK, 20 August 2010.

'Top Ten Questions College Students Ask About God and the Christian Faith,' Cruatunc.com/hp_Wordpress, August 2013.

Verwer, George. *Messiology*. Moody Publishers, 2016.

Wade, Nicholas. 'Finch DNA Shows Darwin Was Right', *The New York Times*, 11 May 1999.

Wallace, J. Warner. 'Perhaps the Greatest Old Testament Prophecy of All', in *Cold Case Christianity*, 8 March 2019.

Williams, Peter J. *Can We Trust the Gospels?* Crossway Books, 30 November 2018.

'Young Earth Creationism, Creation Science and Intelligent Design.' A Statement by the Geological Society of London. Approved by Council 10 April, and published 11 April 2008.

Zukeran, Patrick. *The Dead Sea Scrolls Shed Light on the Accuracy of Our Bible*. Probe Ministries, April 2006.

Websites

Aberystwyth University. '100 Years of Plant Breeding'. https://www.aber.ac.uk/en/ibers/about-us/history/100-years-of-plant-breeding/

Alexander, Denis R. 'Can a Christian Believe in Evolution?' Evangelical Alliance. Last modified 1 May 2005, https://www.eauk.org/church/resources/theological-articles/can-a-christian-believe-in-evolution.cfm.

Applegate, Kathryn. 'Why I Think Adam Was a Real Person in History', BioLogos. Last modified 11 June 2018.

Cauchi, Tony. The Revival Library. https://www.revival-library.org

Cook, Faith. 'Of Whom the World Was Not Worthy – Robert Thomas,' *Evangelical Times*, September 1997. https://www.evangelical-times.org/articles/historical/of-whom-the-world-was-not-worthy-2/

Couchman, D. 'The Mass of the Proton and the Neutron as an Example of Fine Tuning For Life in God'. *New Evidence*, May 2011. http://www.focus.org.uk/proton_neutron.php

Dowd, Mary. 'How Does Embryology Provide Evidence for Evolution?' Sciencing.com, accessed 28 May 2022, https://sciencing.com/how-does-embryology-provide-evidence-for-evolution-13719067.html.

Edwards, 'Dave. A Spiritual Awakening was Taking Place in Rhos – Welsh Revival 1904–5,' Wrexham History. https://www.wrexham-history.com/the-1904–5-welsh-revival/

Friederich, Simon. 'Fine-Tuning', The Stanford Encyclopaedia of Philosophy. Last modified 12 November 2021, https://plato.stanford.edu/entries/fine-tuning/

Gaebelein, Arno C. 'Fulfilled Prophecy a Potent Argument for the Bible,' in *The Fundamentals*, ed. R. A. Torrey. https://www.blueletterbible.org/Comm/torrey_ra/fundamentals/25.cfm

Gellene, Denise. 'Frederick Sanger, 95, Twice a Nobel Laureate and a Genetic Pioneer, Dies.' *The New York Times*, 20 November 2013. https://www.nytimes.com/2013/11/21/science/frederick-sanger-two-time-nobel-winning-scientist-dies-at-95.html

Gonzalez, Eliezer. 'The Story of Robert Thomas – Martyr in Korea,' Good News Unlimited, 31 March 2020. https://www.goodnewsunlimited.com/the-story-of-robert-thomas-martyr-in-korea/

Haarsma, D., and L. Haarsma, 'Comparing Interpretations of Genesis 1', BioLogos. Last modified 9 January 2008, https://biologos.org/articles/comparing-interpretations-of-genesis-1

Ingebritsen, Tom. 'Does Genesis 1 Teach Modern Science?' InterVarsity Emerging Scholars Network. Last modified 15 January 2014, https://blog.emergingscholars.org/2014/01/does-genesis-1-teach-modern-science/

Ingebritsen, Tom. 'The Message of Genesis 1', InterVarsity Emerging Scholars Network. Last modified 9 January 2014, https://blog.emergingscholars.org/2014/01/message-genesis-1/

Johnson, Ben. 'The Last Invasion of Britain', Historic UK. Accessed 15 February 2016, https://www.historic-uk.com/HistoryUK/HistoryofWales/The-Last-Invasion-of-Britain/

Lehmann, Michael. 'Theology Before Darwin: Defusing the Dilemma', BioLogos. Last modified 4 September 2019, https://biologos.org/articles/theology-before-darwin-defusing-the-dilemma.

Masci, David. 'For Darwin Day, 6 Facts About the Evolution Debate', Pew Research Centre. Last modified 11 February 2019, https://www.pewresearch.org/fact-tank/2019/02/11/darwin-day/

Murphy, J. Brendan, and Tjeerd H. Andel, 'Plate Tectonics', *Encyclopedia Britannica*, accessed 15 November 2021, https://www.britannica.com/science/plate-tectonics

O'Dea, Father Frank. 'Our Goldilocks Universe', in Eucharist: the Basic Spirituality, https://theeucharist.wordpress.com/our-goldilocks-universe/

Pike, David Edward. 'Outbreak of Revival in North Pembrokeshire in 1904'. Last modified 10 February 2012. https://www.daibach-welldigger.blogspot.com/2012/02/revival-in-north-pembrokeshire-in-1904.html.

Powell, B. A. 'Explore As Much As We Can': Nobel Prize Winner Charles Townes on

Evolution, Intelligent Design, and the Meaning of Life', UC Berkeley News. Last modified 17 June 2005. https://newsarchive.berkeley.edu/news/media/releases/2005/06/17_townes.shtml

Rogers, Kara. '7 Vestigial Features of the Human Body', *Encyclopedia Britannica*, accessed 15 November 2021, https://www.britannica.com/list/7-vestigial-features-of-the-human-body

'Royal Society Issues Statement on Evolution', NCSE (National Center for Science Education). Last modified 13 April 2006, https://ncse.ngo/royal-society-issues-statement-evolution

Stewart, D. 'How Has God Revealed Himself To Humanity?' Blue Letter Bible, https://www.blueletterbible.org/faq/don_stewart/don_stewart_293.cfm

Swearingen, Chet and Phyllis. The Welsh Revival of 1904–05. Beautiful Feet Inc, IN 46706, USA. March 2018. https://www. romans1015.com/welsh-revival-1904–05/.

Tarr, Leslie K. 'A Prayer Meeting that Lasted 100 Years,' Christian History. https://www.christianhistoryinstitute.org/magazine/article/one-hundred-year-prayer-meeting.

Temming, Maria 'What Is the Age of the Universe?' *Sky and Telescope*. Last modified 18 July 2014, https://skyandtelescope.org/astronomy-resources/age-of-the-universe/

Wikipedia: https://en.wikipedia.org/wiki/Robert_Jermain_Thomas

PLEASE HELP ME BY LEAVING A REVIEW!

I would be very grateful if you could leave a review of this book. Your feedback will be helpful both for myself and for others as they consider reading this book. Please leave your review on the Amazon or other website from where you have bought this. Thank you!

My email address for correspondence is:

rhwillcolchester1@gmail.com